SMART SQUASH

Jahangir Khan (Pakistan) and Anthony Hill (Australia).

SMART SQUASH

**How
to
Win
at
Soft
Ball**

AUSTIN M. FRANCIS

Lyons & Burford, Publishers

To the next Mark Talbott—
may he, or she, honor the soft ball
with the same excellence and dignity
that Mark did for the hard ball.

Printed in the United States of America

Book design by Cindy LaBreacht.

Computerized court projections by Michael Wurmfeld, A.I.A.
Illustrations of grip, stroke, and players in court diagrams by Carol
Fabricatore. Illustrations on pages 109, 113, and 115 by Michael Witte.
Photographs by Viktor Von Dracek, while on assignment for *Squash
News*.

10 9 8 7 6 5 4 3 2 1

Francis, Austin M.
    Smart Squash : how to win at soft ball / Austin M. Francis.
        p.   cm.
    ISBN 1-55821-384-8. — ISBN 1-55821-341-4 (pbk.)
    1. Squash rackets (Game) I. Title
GV1004.F72   1995
796.34′3—dc20   95-7794
                                                                   CIP

Throughout this book the pronouns "he," "him," and "his" are used
inclusively and are intended to apply to both males and females.

All descriptions of shots and tactics are written with right-handed
players in mind.

CONTENTS

INTRODUCTION

After twenty-nine years of playing North American, or hard-ball, squash, I became one of the thousands of players who surrendered to the international soft ball—that squishy, mushy nothing of a ball that has invaded our red-blooded, all-American sport. There were so few hard-ballers left, I had no choice if I wanted to keep playing squash.

Now, eighteen months later, I have made my peace with the soft ball. Worse yet, from one of my die-hard(ball) friend's perspective, I have come to love it. And, as I did years ago for the hard ball, I have written a book about it.

The purpose then—in *Smart Squash: Using Your Head to Win*—was to provide a mental framework for overcoming distractions and playing a focused game. The purpose now is more ambitious. Because soft-ball squash is so completely different, and especially because the majority of American squash players grew up with the hard ball, I faced the need to write a from-the-ground-up, how-to manual.

Moreover, when pitted against native soft-ballers, our American players are embarrassingly inept. The men can't even qualify for the big international tournaments, and the women barely make it past the first round. What are we going to do about it? I hope this book provides an answer. To the extent that it does, its purpose is to provide a road map to American parity with the rest of the squash world.

The German philosopher Georg Hegel believed that you cannot know a thing well without knowing its opposite. As I progressed in the task of defining the soft-ball game in the ways it differs from hard ball, it gave me reason to hope—perhaps hubristically so—that I have provided a sharper focus on the game than has existed up to now, in that it forced me to explain why the techniques and strategies of soft-ball squash are the way they are.

If that is true, maybe my book will have a market among our international squash mentors, whom we now so eagerly imitate.

—Austin M. Francis
Spring, 1995

CONTRIBUTORS

The job of writing a book on soft-ball squash seemed simpler at first than it turned out to be. I had already written one squash book by interviewing seven expert players, coaches, and professionals. So I thought the same amount of effort would work again until I got into my research and discovered how big the differences are—in both degree and kind—between the hard-ball and soft-ball games.

The opportunities—and the need—to understand and explain these differences grew as I progressed, helped certainly by the enthusiasm of each new contributor. Before the process was over, I had talked with nearly four times as many people as I did in the first book. I believe that the result is a thorough treatment of the soft-ball game and that collectively my expert contributors have given me the key to winning soft ball. Here they are, with my sincere gratitude to each:

Paul Assaiante, coach of men's squash at Trinity College, former squash professional at The Princeton Club of New York, tennis author, former national doubles champion with Gordy Anderson in the 40+ age group.

Satinder Bajwa, North American business manager for Jansher Khan, former coach at West Point Military Academy, teaching professional, and champion 35+ soft-ball player.

David Behm, professor of rehabilitation science and exercise physiology, head coach of squash at McGill University, and top-ranked Quebec squash player.

Eliot Berry, one of the first Americans to convert to the soft-ball game, played several years in the British Open in the late 1970s, and was the No. 1 player on the U.S. soft-ball team competing in the World Championships in Canada in 1977.

Craig Brand, executive director of the U.S. Squash Racquets Association, leader in the effort to raise American squash to international standards.

Bob Callahan, coach of men's squash at Princeton University and leader in the switch from hard ball to soft ball among U.S. colleges.

Goldie Edwards, perennial top player in the women's ranks and professor of health and physical education at the University of Pittsburgh.

Ned Edwards, coach of men's squash at the University of Pennsylvania and former touring professional on the hard-ball circuit.

Walter Eichelberger, Jr., in his association with The West Company and Merco—two ball manufacturers—was the creator of the 70+ ball and then a soft ball that became the international standard for several years.

Emily Goodfellow, former coach of women's squash at Princeton University.

Richard Hankinson, assistant coach of women's squash at Princeton University, former county champion from Surrey, England, editor of a demographic research journal in the Office of Population Research, Princeton University.

Demer Holleran, coach of women's squash at the University of Pennsylvania, No. 1 U.S. women's soft-ball player, currently ranked No. 27 in women's world soft ball.

Quentin Hyder, physician and long-time soft-ball enthusiast, established and ran the first formal soft-ball tournament in the U.S.

Hazel and Tom Jones, publishers of *Squash News,* the official newspaper for squash in the U.S., originators in 1985 of the U.S. Open championships, which introduced world-class soft-ballers to the U.S., founders in 1989 of the International Grand Prix, which since its inception has featured international players in eighty-three events across the U.S.

Brett Martin, world No. 2 soft-ball player from Australia, member of the famed squash-playing Martin family that includes his brother Rodney and sister Michelle.

Jay Nelson, highly ranked U.S. amateur player, currently plays both a hard-ball season and a soft-ball season, winning many tournaments with each ball.

Peter Nicol, newcomer to the top ranks of world soft ball, originally from Scotland, now playing out of London, winner of the 1994 Rolex U.S. Open.

John Nimick, executive director of the world Professional Squash Association and director of the popular Lehman Brothers Tournament of Champions, which brings top international players to New York City.

David Pearson, world champion in the 35+ age group (former top 15 in open class), private coach to many world-class adult and junior players, squash professional from Harrowgate, England.

Neil Pomphrey, assistant coach of men's squash at Princeton University, began playing in Scotland, a top-ranked 35+ men's soft-ball player, principal research physicist at Princeton University's Plasma Physics Laboratory.

Frank Satterthwaite, professor of management at Johnson & Wales University, former touring professional on the hard-ball circuit, squash author, member of the first U.S. soft-ball team at the World Championships in Africa.

Mark Talbott, long-time No. 1 hard-ball professional in the U.S., coach of the U.S. boys team, founder of the Talbott Squash Academy, a squash training center in Rhode Island dedicated to developing U.S. junior players.

Craig Thorpe-Clark, director of the U.S. Squash Racquets Association's National Coaching Development program, coach of the U.S. women's team, holder of a Level 3 coaching certification of the British Squash Rackets Association.

Gary Waite, recent No. 1 North American professional soft-ball player, from Toronto, also plays on the hard-ball tour.

I have benefited greatly from three excellent books by international players and coaches and their deep understanding of squash (for them there is no distinction between "hard" and "soft"—it's just *squash*). I highly recommend these books:

Jahangir Khan with Richard Eaton, *Go and Play Squash: Techniques and Tactics,* Stanley Paul, London, 1992.

Ian McKenzie, *The Squash Workshop: A Complete Game Guide,* The Crowood Press Ltd., Ramsbury, Marlborough, 1992.

Eric Sommers, *Squash: Technique, Tactics, Training,* The Crowood Press Ltd., 1991.

Several individuals deserve special credit:

Paul Assaiante and **Bob Callahan**, who gave me their wisdom in interviews, read the manuscript, and provided advice and support throughout the project.

Lilly Golden, my editor at Lyons & Burford, who not only saw what was missing, but was also the book's chief expediter amongst all the parties, occasional diplomat, and gentle taskmaster when it was necessary.

Nancy Morin, my co-worker at A. M. Francis Inc., who transcribed nearly 1,000 pages of interviews and enthusiastically supported the creation of the book even as it borrowed from our company's time.

Michael Wurmfeld, squash player and architect, who placed his firm's computer-assisted design system at my disposal and advised on its use, and his associate **Mario Censullo**, who then created the court projections for the shot and drill diagrams.

The shot and drill diagrams are unusual in that they required five essential elements, each indispensable to their creation: the architecturally correct court projections just mentioned; the player positions and shot trajectories carefully worked out with my expert contributors; the photographs I took of **Paul Assaiante** and **Eliot Berry** posed in each of the player positions; the art illustrations by **Carol Fabricatore** of Paul and Eliot "hitting" their shots inside the court projections; and, finally, the financial support to underwrite Carol's drawings, so generously donated by **Brent Nicklas**, on behalf of **Landmark Partners Inc.**, and **Leo Pierce, Jr.**, and his family company **Pierce Leahy**

Archives. Squash, as a niche sport, depends for its well-being and growth on the generosity of individuals like Leo and Brent, who often are both avid players and successful business people, vitally interested in the advancement of our favorite game.

Peter Nicol (Scotland) and Damian Walker (U.S.A.).

1. FOR NEWCOMERS TO THE GAME

Squash is a wonderfully compact sport. It fits into busy lives, small spaces, and moderate budgets. It provides great exercise in just 30 to 45 minutes, is intensely competitive, mentally stimulating, can be played year-round indoors, and is highly social. Squash is an ideal sport for urban athletes.

As you rush out the door to sign up for lessons, here are a few essentials about the game. Squash is a game played with a soft rubber ball in a small white room using a lightweight, strung racquet. It is most often compared with tennis except for two major differences—the containing walls and the fact that you must share the same space with your opponent.

The walls make squash a game of angles, something like billiards played in three dimensions. Moreover, you don't aim directly at your target, you rebound the ball off at least one wall to your target. These angled shots challenge the retriever to position himself for and intercept a ball that keeps changing direction each time it hits a wall. For the striker, the angles offer an expanded repertory of shot choices, not the least of which is the game-defining *boast*.

Sharing the same space as your opponent adds a mix of psychological pressure, rigorous etiquette, and, occasionally, physical danger. The rules governing interference with an opponent's shot are a key factor in the progress of a match. All in all, squash is an exhilarating game whose essence has been described best by Bill Robinson, a New York area writer who has played squash for some sixty years, in an article that appeared in the *New York Times:* "That half hour of intense concentration on the little black ball zinging around four white walls like a drunken bumblebee is the greatest antidote there is for whatever bugs you about the rest of the world. Squash releases tensions and aggressions, works out poisons, gives the most concentrated workout you can get for the time spent, keeps you out of three-martini lunches, supposedly improves your sex life—and is also just plain fun. It literally has 'all the angles,' and fanatics like me feel that its complex fascinations are unmatched in the racquet world."

In spite of its complexities, squash is conceptually quite simple: you must hit the front wall with the ball between the "tin" and the out-of-court line (see Figures 1 and 2) and retrieve your opponent's shot on the fly or before the ball bounces twice. The ball may go directly to the front wall or indirectly there after hitting the back or side walls. The rally ends when the ball has bounced twice, gone out of court, or when the ball hits the floor on the way from the striker's racquet to the front wall.

After a five-minute warmup, the serve is determined by spinning the racquet, the winner choosing to serve from either service box. The server continues as long as he wins the rally, alternating service boxes after each point. When the receiver wins the rally, he becomes the server, choosing which side to start serving from, and so on. The serve must hit the front wall above the cut line and bounce, unless volleyed by the receiver, in the opposite rear quarter of the court. The server has one serve and in the case of a fault, loses the serve. The winner of a game serves first in the next game. A 90-second rest period is permitted between games.

A match is won by the player who first wins three games. The nine-point international scoring system is used in most cases, where a point can be scored only on the serve. The player who scores nine points first wins the game. At eight-all, the play-

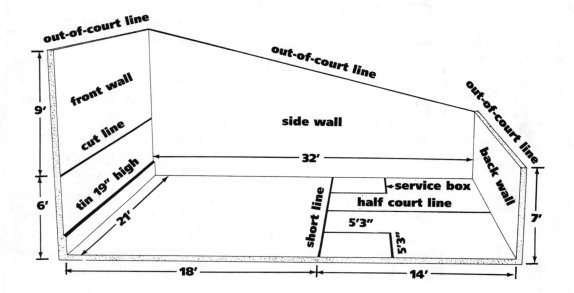

Fig. 1. International (Soft Ball) Squash Court

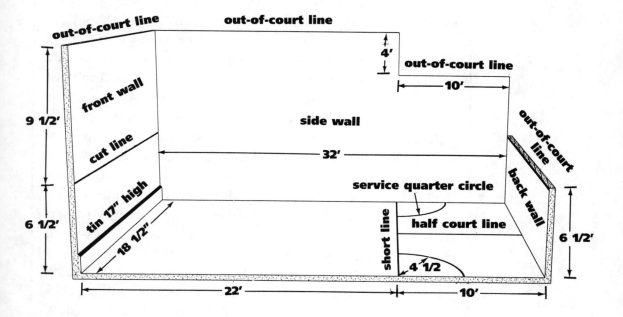

Fig. 2. North American (Hard Ball) Squash Court

er who already had eight points has two choices: 1) to play one more point, in which case he calls "no set," or 2) to play two more points, in which case he calls "set two."

Alternatively, if the 15-point scoring system is used, at 14-all the player who reached 14 points first has a choice of "no set" to 15 points or "set three" to 17 points. The 15-point matches are also won by whoever wins three games first. The 15-point scoring system is being adopted more frequently for exhibition matches and at tournaments to shorten match times and give spectators the satisfaction of watching points being scored on each rally.

The point of entry into the squash world might be a school with a coach and squash team or a club with a squash professional and an organized program of play. As squash becomes more egalitarian in America, court facilities are springing up outside the prep school, private university, private club environment. With its increasing public accessibility and the relative ease of learning afforded by the switch to the soft ball, squash is gaining popularity as a source of fitness and competitive recreation.

At the beginning levels of competition, you find intraclub ladders and tournaments, followed by interclub leagues and team matches. The skill levels nationwide are A, B, C, and D, for both women and men, with occasionally an E, or novice, level in larger metropolitan areas. A is the highest amateur level, usually dominated by ex-varsity alumni players from the 40-odd colleges with active squash programs.

Beyond the club leagues are the tournaments, usually held on weekends and run by the clubs, or by local, regional, or national associations. There are tournaments for all skill levels and veteran's age groups beginning at 35 and going up in five-year increments until one that was added just recently for 85-year-old players!

In New York City, the Metropolitan Squash Racquets Association oversees some seven leagues involving forty-seven teams, in what has become almost totally soft-ball competition.

The governing body of squash in America is the U.S. Squash Racquets Association: P.O. Box 1216, 23 Cynwyd Road, Bala Cynwyd, PA 19004, Telephone: (610) 667-4006, Fax: (610) 667-6539. Craig Brand, executive director of the USSRA, runs a small office of a half-dozen people with the large mission of directing the growth of squash into a nationally unified, broad-based sports program.

The USSRA has the additional goal of bringing the caliber of U.S. squash up to the world standard. This is a particularly stiff challenge, as the U.S. has so recently switched from the hard ball to the soft ball used by the rest of the squash-playing world for the entire 150-year existence of the game. A big step forward in this mission was the gathering in 1995 of squash players from North and South America in Mar del Plata, Argentina, for the Pan American Games, where squash was included for the first time as an official sport. And there is the further prospect that squash, in the not-too-distant future, might become an Olympic sport.

In the realm of U.S. squash communications, there is only one consistent and reliable source of news, and that is *Squash News*. Begun in 1978 by Hazel and Tom Jones and published continuously since then, *Squash News* is an independently published monthly newspaper devoted entirely to squash. For subscription or other information, Hazel and Tom can be reached at 186 Arcadia Road, Hope Valley, RI 02832, Telephone: (401) 539-2381, Fax: (401) 539-2490. Membership in the USSRA automatically includes a subscription to *Squash News*.

At the world level, the governing body for squash is the World Squash Federation, of which the USSRA is a founding member. The WSF can be reached at 6 Havelock Road, Hastings TN34 1BP, Great Britain.

The world's touring professional players are organized under the aegis of the Professional Squash Association, 82 Cathedral Road, Cardiff CFI 9LN, Wales, Great Britain. The PSA, run by John Nimick, sanctions and schedules professional tournaments, the best known of which in the U.S. is the Lehman Brothers Tournament of Champions, usually held in April in New York City. PSA/USA can be reached at 56 Spooner Road, Chestnut Hill, MA 02167, Telephone: (617) 731-6874, Fax: (617) 277-1457.

The WSF estimates that there are now 15 million players and almost 45,000 courts in 112 countries, and that squash is one of the fastest growing sports in the world.

Ned Edwards (U.S.A.) and Mark Talbott (U.S.A.).

2. THE STATE OF AMERICAN SQUASH

THE END OF A CENTURY-OLD TRADITION

"The soft-ball revolution has come extremely fast," says Bob Callahan, coach of men's squash at Princeton University. "I can't think of another revolution of a sport that within a space of five years has gone from a little group playing soft ball to taking over the sport."

The impact of switching to the soft ball carries far beyond the physical differences between the two balls to the economics, politics, player performance, and ultimately to the standing of American squash among the 112 squash-playing nations of the world. Only three countries—Canada, the United States, and Mexico—ever played hard ball, and Canada switched to the soft ball ten years ago. The rest of the world, since squash began in England, has always played with the soft ball.

With our 100-year-old tradition of hard ball, which everyone agrees is a totally different game, why did we change? For that matter, how did the two versions of squash evolve separately in the first place?

The origins of squash are poorly recorded. The earliest mention of it in a book appears nearly fifty years after it was first played. Squash was "discovered" at Harrow in 1822 by boys "getting their eye in" as they waited their turn to play *rackets*. The three-sided space outside the larger rackets court was too small for the hard and much faster rackets ball, so the boys used a soft rubber ball instead, and the "squashy" sound of the impact of that ball gave the game its name.

Until 1922, there was no organized squash competition or governing body in England, so for nearly one hundred years the game was played in courts of varying dimensions depending upon the space available, with balls of different size and rebound, and without generally accepted rules. Courts were built in the country houses of old Harrovians, in the British army outposts in India, and in London's West End clubs, sixteen of which had squash courts by 1930. In 1922, the Tennis and Rackets Association adopted squash and standardized the court dimensions at 21 by 32 feet, a size supposedly based on Lord Desborough's private court. The earliest British squash league, the Bath Club Cup, began with the 1922-23 season. Ball standards were not established until 1928, when the Squash Rackets Association was founded.

In the United States, the first squash court was built in 1882 at St. Paul's School, Concord, New Hampshire with specifications imported from Montreal. The soft ball—because of its mushy, dead bounce—was far too slow for the New England winters, so a harder, faster ball was used, as well as a heavier racquet to hit it with. (Incidentally, the spelling of "racquet" probably also came from French-speaking Canadians along with the court dimensions.) Following the pattern in England, American squash evolved in the private universities and then the city clubs. The first club courts appeared simultaneously in 1891 at the Racquet Club of Philadelphia and at the Racquet & Tennis Club in New York City, at its 43rd Street location.

Squash thrived in the Northeast from the early 1900s. The first U.S. amateur championship was held in 1908, and our national association was formed around 1919, when the standard court dimensions were set at 18 1/2 by 32 feet. John Iole, a Pittsburgh attorney, wrote in a historical article on squash, "Squash originally was known simply as 'squash' everywhere but the United States. The U.S. employed the term 'squash racquets' to distinguish the game from squash tennis, a remarkably obscure racket game played in a slightly smaller court [17 by 32 feet] than hard-ball squash and with rosewood-finished walls, using chopped-down tennis rackets and a special ball."

Thus soft-ball and hard-ball squash were formalized separately, an ocean apart, and they stayed apart for the next 60 to 70 years. English and American squash players communicated from time to time, and attempts were made to bring the two games together. There is a story that the British decided in 1911 that they should teach the Americans how to play the proper game. So their Squash Rackets Association sent an emissary to tell us about the real game, the wider court, the softer ball. Everything was set except for one unforeseeable mistake. He came on the Titanic.

An English team is reported to have toured the U.S. in 1924, but the great differences in the two games prevented any reciprocal tour in England. As far as we know, the idea of integrating the games did not resurface until 1935 when the Americans again followed the English by establishing a Jesters group, social squash players who play each other once a year. The British/American Jesters' matches and the inevitable jibes over each other's version of squash were the beginnings of an ongoing discussion about integrating the two games.

The first actual soft-ball event in the U.S. took place in 1969 when Quentin Hyder, ex-Cambridge squasher who had come to this country to practice medicine, was asked by some friends at the New York Athletic Club to organize a soft-ball tournament. He put together a draw of sixteen players, and the following year was asked if he would run "his" tournament again. It took hold, came to be known as the Hyder Invitational, and progressively added a professional division, a women's division, age groups, then a B division, and in 1994 attracted over 120 players in the various divisions. In 1974, the Hyder tournament moved to

Harry Saint's Uptown Racquet Club, where two 21-foot courts had just been built, thought to be the first wide courts in the United States.

SOFT BALL'S INEXORABLE TAKEOVER

In the late 1960s, squash players in the Northeast started playing with the soft ball as a summer substitute to the hard ball, which was much too fast when it overheated on the then mostly un-air-conditioned courts.

The soft ball's appeal was not limited to its suitability in hot courts. Soft-ball leagues formed, initially for a three-month summer season, then gradually the season expanded. By the early 1990s, the soft ball had become so popular that many players were saying, "We enjoy the soft ball more, and we're not changing back."

There has been a lot of grief and controversy over the revolution in North American squash. Some veteran hard-ballers have accused the soft-ball forces of organizing a coup. Bob Callahan thinks, however, that "this whole move to soft ball is completely customer-driven. There is nobody holding a gun to anyone's head saying, 'You have to play soft ball.' It's happened on its own. It's simply the ball of choice."

I asked Bob if he thinks the possibility of having squash become an Olympic sport is a driving force in the American switch to the soft ball. He commented on the political and financial hurdles that still have to be cleared before we have a chance to make the Olympics. "More important," he said, "there may be eight or ten kids all over the U.S. who are thinking of playing in the Olympics, but the thousands and thousands of others who are playing soft ball are not playing it because they are going to play in the Olympics. So I think that incentive or argument is a non-factor. It makes it more genuine that this country's moving to soft ball even without the assurance that an Olympic opportunity is imminent."

The takeover by soft ball has penetrated virtually every precinct of American squash.

■ The 1993 Rolex U.S. National Soft Ball Championships in San Francisco set an attendance record of 628 players—nearly 200 players had to be turned away—surpassing hard ball's old record of 576 players in the U.S. National Hard Ball Championships in Philadelphia in 1987.

■ In April 1994, the U.S. Squash Racquets Association recommended to its board that the North American Open, long considered "the Wimbledon of hard-ball squash," be switched to a soft-ball event.

■ U.S. women college players switched in 1993—the 1993 Howe Cup, the national women's intercollegiate team championships, changed from hard ball to soft ball and drew a record number of teams.

■ The men's intercollegiate representatives (of 33 colleges) voted to switch to soft ball beginning with the 1994-95 season.

■ Prep schools in the Northeast switched permanently to soft ball with the 1993-94 season. The first year was pronounced "a rousing success" by coaches and players.

■ Junior players in the U.S. switched permanently to soft ball with the beginning of the 1994 season, so that any U.S. junior who starts squash from now on will learn soft ball. They will be the first pure, home-grown soft-ballers.

The most accurate reflection of the switch to soft ball lies in the sales statistics of Dunlop/Slazenger, maker of the best-selling hard and soft balls. Their U.S. soft-ball sales passed hard ball in 1991 and have been widening the gap since then. In the first six months of 1994, Dunlop's soft balls outsold their hard balls 10 to 1.

I asked Demer Holleran, who has dominated women's hard ball in the U.S. for the past few years, if she is sorry to see it dying out. "I guess I'm sad to see it die, but I'm also a realist. I think it's the best thing. You could say I had a lot to lose by seeing it die. I probably did, I mean Ned Edwards did, along with a lot of the other hard-ball players with good years of competitive play still ahead of them. But you have to look at the thing long term. It's the best thing for the game. It's the best thing for the sport in our country because soft ball is a great sport."

Mark Talbott reflected on his career in hard-ball and how the game is dwindling in popularity: "The hard-ball surge kind of followed my career. It just started taking off in the early 80s and it really got big in the mid 80s. There was a big professional tour then. I was lucky to have been there at the right time, my timing was good, it was exciting. It's a strange feeling for me that I'm really sort of being forced into retirement. I'm only planning on playing for another year or so anyway, so I feel fortunate. I feel a little sad for some of the younger players, like Marcos Mendez, Rodolfo Rodriguez. Those two could have done quite well on the tour, but there's really nothing for them now, they're decent soft-ball players, but they're never going to be great the way they are in hard ball, it's too hard for them to catch up. Hard ball is just fading out, there's going to be no player base any more."

John Nimick, executive director of the North American division of the worldwide Professional Squash Association, commented on the effect that switching to soft ball has had on the American touring professionals. "The U.S. pros have had a crisis of sorts, in all honesty and reality. The last group of U.S. pros was Ned, Mark, and me. We were it, we had a living, a career, we had excitement, we had a tour. But we were all relatively lucky, to reach the point where we were old enough not to need that tour any more, and to move on to other things. Whereas a pro like Jeff Stanley, who was ready to dominate the tour, got left in the cold."

What is going to happen to the hard-ball game? It gets progressively harder to put together a full draw in the hard-ball events, and the number of such events is shrinking. There are still a lot of excellent hard-ball players, and the USSRA is committed to supporting hard-ball events as long as there is a demand for them. The sad reality is, however—and it is sad—that hard ball is history. It will stay around as long as there are age-group tournaments, but eventually, in a sort of actuarial decline, it will die. And we'll be left with the legacy of narrow courts for years to come.

THE APPEALS OF SOFT BALL

Besides the traditional and continuing appeals of squash as an ideal urban sport, soft-ball squash has further appeals that inevitably led to its replacement of hard ball.

Soft ball is easier to learn. Richard Hankinson, a former champion of Surrey County, England, who has taught many youngsters to play, says, "Kids coming up from seven and eight onwards love the soft ball because it is a nice, bouncy ball that suits their ability. They can keep the ball going almost from the first day. In the old days, we used to put the kids on the court with the hard ball and it would be serve, end of point, serve, end of point. It took them until they were in their teens before they could get a reasonable game with the hard ball." Goldie Edwards, long-time top female player in the U.S., agrees: "I hate to say this, but for women as well as kids, because the hard ball flies around so, it really is off-putting, and the softer ball, where you can actually *loop* it up—which is good basic squash anyway—that really makes getting into squash easier."

Soft ball's longer rallies are a better workout and more fun. It's clear that you do more running in soft ball, because the slower ball keeps you in the point. But the rewards go beyond the exercise factor; there is also the exhilaration of a great exchange of shots. It is ironic that long rallies are now seen as a benefit, because U.S. players used to criticize the soft-ball game as being a "mindless endurance contest."

Soft ball is physically less damaging. Jay Nelson, a top U.S. amateur who plays both balls in season, says, "Hard ball is more likely to lead to shoulder and back injuries than soft ball because of the jerking. When I switch from soft ball back to hard ball, I usually wind up early on with some lower back problems." Mark Talbott, long the professional hard-ball champion of North America, agrees: "Hard ball at the very best level is as physically demanding and sometimes more so than soft ball because you're jerked around so quickly and it takes such a toll on your body. Teaching pros tell me they much prefer teaching soft ball because they can kind of lope around the court when they're giving lessons." According to Ned Edwards, who coaches the men's team at the University of Pennsylvania, "There's something more gentle about it. It's more friendly, not just for the beginner but for everyone."

Soft ball rewards timing, patience, and the careful shot over raw power. These qualities appeal to women players. You get a better look at the ball, more time to set up and hit a controlled shot. Quentin Hyder, long-time American soft-ball enthusiast, says, "The hard ball required faster reaction times, quicker reflexes, so veterans had a harder time keeping up with it, and there were far fewer exchanges per rally. The longer time between shots [in soft ball] enables any player to play a more thinking game, more time to play the shot correctly, unhurriedly, and with more thought to both tactics and strategy."

Soft ball allows more deception in the choice of shots. Again, because you have more time to get ready, you can hit a greater variety of shots off the same preparation. As Paul Assaiante, coach of men's squash at Trinity College, says, "Soft ball allows you to blend your shotmaking, so you can go to the front wall and make the drive and the drop shot look the same, the starting points look the same." I asked Jay Nelson if he thinks deception is a factor in soft ball. He says, "Big, big. Maybe you don't win the point, but you go up and show one shot and hit another. These guys will delay their shot, put you on hold, and really hurt you." Frank Satterthwaite, former top-ranked hardball professional and squash author, says: "I had a reputation as being a shotmaker, always looking to put the ball away, and so you would think that soft ball would really be frustrating for me but, actually, setting up fakes is very appealing to me, and in soft ball you have time to do that, to lift your racquet way up then dip it down and hit a drop shot. I have the pleasure of putting a whole lot of different moves on you."

"Soft ball is a wonderful game." So says Emily Goodfellow, former coach of women's squash at Princeton University. "I believe that more often in soft ball than in hard ball the better player wins. I think it's a fairer game. By better player I mean a more complete player. You have to have very sound strokes and good balance. To drive the ball around the court, you can't be off balance. You can't have something funky going on in your swing. You have to know the game. You have to have a very good understanding of strategy. There's not a whole lot of luck involved. And

I think you have to be in good physical condition. In soft ball, to win you have to be pretty high up in at least two of the three areas of technique, strategy, and conditioning."

THE AMERICAN CHALLENGE

If America is going to play even with the rest of the soft-ball world, what will it take to get there? At this writing, our best male player is ranked No. 131 worldwide, our top female is No. 27, and our junior boys team just returned from New Zealand, where it finished 21 out of 27 teams.

Estimates by the leaders in American squash of how long it will take to produce an American soft-ball champion range from four to twenty years. My own estimate centers on the yet-to-be-identified handful of 10-year-olds who have already played mostly soft ball and who will make it to the top in eight to ten years if they dedicate themselves to the championship regimen laid out in other sections of this book.

At the outset, the squash community must provide an environment in which champions can thrive. This means the further spread nationwide of urban squash centers similar to those that have already been established in Atlanta and San Francisco, where good players can find plenty of competition. John Nimick believes that "for us to get to the top in world soft ball, it will take five or six very strong local, integrated soft-ball communities, cities with 10 to 20 courts, and a dynamic junior program."

Speaking of the goals of the U.S. Squash Racquets Association, its executive director, Craig Brand, emphasizes the indispensability of a strong junior program. "We are becoming more international now, we were in the 1995 Pan American Games, we are pursuing a place in the Olympic Games, which would of course be soft ball. We are after recognition and elevation of the sport to full medal status, and with that comes revenue. Revenue, in turn, funds great programs for juniors, so it's a gradual process of building up our sport."

There will need to be a growing number of commercial facilities where anyone can play, with the goal of enlarging the customer base and developing a broader supply of players. Squash must shake the bonds of its prep school, Ivy League, private club heritage. Those institutions will continue to be at the core of the sport, but they must not be its majority.

The successful commercial facility, in addition to providing good squash, will tap the demand for fitness combined with an ambiance conducive to socializing. Happily for this scenario, the soft ball makes for much more even match-ups between male and female players than the hard ball ever could.

Craig Brand tells a story that illustrates how squash is moving away from being dominated by white-collar professionals. "When the University of Minnesota put in six beautiful, wide courts, they feared that no one would play. All of a sudden, out of the woodwork came every foreign grad student who had played squash back in his own country—Indians, Pakistanis, Germans. And they came with squash racquets, so that now the courts are used all the time. If institutions want to avoid making a speculative investment, they should go to their grad schools and take a survey to find out how many students have played squash."

I asked Mark Talbott how important it is to make squash attractive on TV and how that relates to getting sponsorship. "For squash to gain sponsorship," he said, "it needs just the numbers. Until we get enough people playing it, it doesn't matter how good we can make it look on TV. We need a big enough base of players to appeal to the sponsors as a market."

In a breakthrough for squash, Mark's squash academy in Newport attracted a grant from the U.S. Olympic Committee for an elite under-19 training program. "It was the first outside money we've gotten to develop the sport. And now, we're building a big, seven-court facility at St. George's School here which has been designated the national training center by the USSRA, for adults and juniors, so things are looking up."

If America is going to catch up with the rest of the squash world, it cannot be done without uniformly high standards of coaching in our schools, clubs, and squash centers. Until recently, the standards and hierarchy of squash coaching in this country have been determined through a process akin to natural selection. The USSRA has begun to upgrade and formalize this process by naming Craig Thorpe-Clark, a British Squash Rackets Association Level 3 coach, as its director of national coaching development and coach of the U.S. women's team.

Thorpe-Clark points out that coaches in other countries must be certified before they can be hired. "In England, you can't get a job at a club unless you're qualified at a certain level. It's true around the world in soft ball. The Level 1 course we have designed for the United States has been approved by the World Squash Federation as being on a par with coaching courses in Australia, England, Finland, New Zealand, and Germany, so the U.S. is now in that program."

Although there is a Level 4, any coaching position is available to a coach certified at Level 3. For a good squash player to go through all three levels of certification would take about five years. Coaching is becoming more scientific, and some coaches at the top levels also have degrees, or have taken courses, in physiology, biomechanics, sports psychology, and other performance-related sciences.

Thorpe-Clark and the USSRA hope soon to begin teaching, in a given year, fifteen Level 1 courses, ten Level 2 courses, and one or two Level 3 courses at selected locations around the country. The Level 1 course takes 20 hours and costs the professional or his employer two hundred dollars. In 1994, there were only three Level 3 coaches in the U.S. (Thorpe-Clark in Bala Cynwyd, Pa., Brian Patterson in New York, and Richard Milburn in Atlanta, all of them British coaches), five or six Level 2's and about 75 or 80 Level 1's.

To develop world-class U.S. players also demands exposure to top-level squash. Hazel and Tom Jones, publishers of *Squash News,* have made great strides toward this end by originating both the U.S. Open championships and the International Grand Prix series, and arranging with Rolex and Head to be their respective sponsors. The Grand Prix series brings world-class players to many U.S. cities, offering both exhibition flights and flights that integrate the best local players, giving them a chance to compete against the top overseas soft-ballers.

Demer Holleran, who made the transition from the No. 1 U.S. female hard-ball player to the No. 1 soft-ball player, thinks that without top role models, we cannot inspire our junior players to greatness. "I always maintain that you can only go as far as your expectations. When I was growing up, my aspiration was to be the best hard-ball player there was. And I only saw Alicia McConnell and the other top hard-ball players, so that's who I aspired to be better than. I didn't see the women's world soft-ball champ Susan Devoy play, so I never had the aspiration to be better than her. For that reason, I think it's really important to show young kids the best there is. They should be seeing the U.S. Open and the world's top players, and then they'll say, 'In 10 years I'm going to be that good.'"

John Nimick, when asked how important he thinks it is to have an American win his premier soft-ball event, the Lehman Brothers Tournament of Champions, answered, "I think it's very important. It's not quite so important now because, with the transition to soft ball so recent, most of the U.S. community wants to see the best in the game. That works within the squash community, but within the non-squash community, to make the game truly popular, you have to have an American champ. There's still a great hill to climb within the squash community in terms of attendance, support, and sponsorship. But for us to get beyond that level, we absolutely have to have an American champion!"

John also had some very interesting thoughts on what the touring professionals are doing to make their product more spectator-friendly. "Even as the U.S. goes to soft ball, PSA worldwide is exploring ways to make soft ball at the professional level more interesting to watch because we recognize that it's not as exciting as say volleyball or even tennis. Matches don't carry the kind of excitement and drama, tension and crisis that they need, and in fact that hard ball used to have. So we're experimenting with playing singles on 25-foot-wide courts. Jansher Khan recently played on a 25-foot court in London and his coach was there and said it was brilliant! Maybe where you score only to five so that each point is really important like in tennis, where, after a very short group of points, you win something. We have lowered the tin already, to encourage more shooting, shorter points. Maybe there should be a shot clock, meaning if you can't win the point within 30 seconds, you lose the serve. However, none of these changes would affect recreational squash."

In the last analysis, the American challenge becomes personal—for the player and for the coach. Demer's goal now is not so much to rise in the rankings, which requires ten tournaments and a lot of travel each year, but to improve her game and represent the U.S. at a better level of performance than her previous personal best. "Coming from hard ball," she says, "there's a totally different psyche that you need to be a soft-ball player. I've played almost all of the top women internationally, although I've yet to beat anyone in the top 16. One thing that comes to mind about all those players is patience. I tend not to have quite as much patience and confidence in my fitness. But I've gotten significantly better with my fitness, and I think I'm maturing as a player."

Asking Ned Edwards if he thinks we need to have help from the British coaches before we can bring our players to the top level evoked an eloquent rejoinder: "In terms of our future and educating our young players with the soft ball, I don't think we have to wait for a cadre of British teachers to come over here to effectively teach us. I think this is about being able to hit drop shots. It's about being able to hit volleys into the nick. It's about being able to drive the ball hard for length. It's about being able to have control of the racquet. These things are not magic. And we don't need a Jonah Barrington to come teach us that.

"Once our American coaches know where this ball needs to end up, I think we can teach our players how to do it. And there have always been different styles of squash. Jonah hit the ball differently than Geoff Hunt hit the ball, than Jahangir Khan hit the ball. So in that same way, the school out of the United States will be a bit different than the school out of Pakistan. I do not feel that in order for us to succeed here we need to wait for enlightenment to come from overseas. We know where the ball needs to go to win points. And so now we teach our players how to hit it there. If we focus on our youngsters who have good talent, it's not as though our genes are inferior here. We can do this. It's an issue of confidence."

Demer Holleran (U.S.A.), foreground, and Ellie Pierce (U.S.A.).

3. IT'S A WHOLE NEW BALL GAME

The parade of different balls in American squash has been relentless. Since the mid-1960s, about every five years or so a new ball has appeared on the scene, each with altogether different playing properties from its predecessor. You had the Cragin- Simplex Green Diamond (a black ball that marked up the white courts terribly and broke "like eggs," according to the professionals who had to provide them); the West-Merco green ball (a non-marking ball); the Seamco "seamless" (a shiny black ball that never really caught on); the West Company 70-plus (a slightly smaller, thinner-walled, and slower ball than the North American hard ball, produced with the thought that it might help bring the soft-ball and hard-ball games together); the Slazenger blue ball with the orange dot (this one caught on and became popular, only to go the way of all the others); the Dunlop fuschia ball with the white dot (some hard-ballers think this one plays like a rock); and now—the Dunlop/Slazenger XX Yellow Dot (the international soft ball).

The ball has always been an orphan in this country, perhaps because squash hasn't been a big enough sport to support the consistent manufacture of a ball that would stay the same over time. Now that the switch to the soft ball is behind us, it would be wonderful if the alignment with 14 million other users worldwide were to contribute to the stability of the ball and eliminate a source of frustration that has plagued North American squash players for years.

At the very least, we now have *one world, one ball!*

To gain a quick idea of the difference between the hard and soft balls, try squeezing each one between thumb and forefinger—you probably can press the two sides of the soft ball together but not even dent the hard ball. As measured by Dunlop/Slazenger, maker of both balls, the soft ball is 10 times more compressible than the hard ball. More important than the compressibility, of course, is the playability.

Frank Satterthwaite makes this analysis: "There are two big differences in the playability of the ball. First, the soft ball's angle-of-bounce is markedly different from that of the hard ball. When the hard ball hits a surface, it tends to come off at the same angle; when the soft ball hits, it flattens, grabs, and tends to come off at more of a right angle. In fact, I call this tendency 'perpendicularity.' This has a number of consequences: if the ball hits the floor, it is going to sit up; if it hits the side wall, it is going to come out towards the center of the court. So every time the ball hits a playing surface, there's a bias towards that ball ending up in the center of the court, which is where you don't want the ball. For amateurs anyway, with either ball, the basic problem is that the ball's always ending up in the center of the court, and that's happening even more so with the soft ball.

"Second, the soft ball's speed is cut dramatically with each impact on a surface. It has been estimated that the soft ball loses 50 percent of its speed with each impact, whereas the hard ball loses only about 25 percent. Because of the perpendicularity and the speed loss, two new demands are placed on the soft-ball player—you have to move to a ball that used to come to you, and your shots must be hit with greater precision. If you hit a rail shot, it has got to be *pure*; it can't hit the side wall or it's just going to come out. And on a cross-court drive, the target on the side wall is critical—not too short or it will bounce out near the service box and not too deep or it can be cut off and volleyed."

A benefit of the soft ball not yet fully appreciated by newcomers is the fact that the ball comes in varying speeds and, although the Dunlop XX Yellow Dot is the usual choice for tournaments, there is no single official ball overseas as there tends to be in the United States. Richard Hankinson noted that "in England, we use any ball that suits the temperature of the court on a given day. The Squash Rackets Association has a temperature chart and if it drops below a certain level, you switch to a faster ball. To judge this just by playing, you should use whatever ball you can hit to the back wall without busting a gut. If you hit it onto the front wall a foot below the service line on a drive and can still get it onto the back wall before it's bounced twice, you're probably playing with the right ball."

Dunlop makes four standard balls going up in speed from yellow, to white, to red, to blue—in each case the color of the small dot on the basic black ball. When Hankinson was teaching in England, they also used a big spongy, orange ball and cutdown racquets to teach 6- to 7-year-olds in a mini-squash program. There are two special balls at the slow end of the spectrum, an orange dot or "desert ball" for very hot courts, and a green dot for high-altitude play.

Frank Satterthwaite adds one other insight on choosing the right ball to play with: "Most people have more fun if they play with the white or red dot rather than the yellow dot. The notion that 'the pros and A players play with the yellow dot, therefore I should do the same' is incorrect. For one thing, the pros often practice with the red dot because it is equivalent to the yellow dot in tournament conditions. Moreover, a slightly faster ball promotes longer rallies and a more exhilarating, beneficial workout at the club level."

And then there's the *wide* court—2 1/2 feet wider than the North American court, with a slanted, much lower side line and a T four feet closer to the front wall—big differences that we will analyze and discuss as they affect tactics and shot choices in the upcoming chapters.

It's fair to say that, between the radically different ball and court, *it's a whole new ball game.* The switchover is complex and should not be underestimated. It alters the fundamentals of the game from *mentality* to *tactics* to *technique.*

Demer Holleran remembers what it was like when she began learning soft ball: "I guess the thing I had the most trouble with was being a shooter. In hard ball, my strength was being quick to the ball and being able to play the angles and to put the ball away as quickly as possible. In soft ball, you can't get away with that as well. You must learn how to play for position, and that is a different mind set. You have to get used to playing for the opening instead of feeling the opening's there on the first loose ball you get. And not shooting off the serve. Shooting off the serve is a huge weakness hard-ball players have. Also, hitting reverse corners rarely wins a point and can put you at a huge disadvantage. Those are hard-ball traps we fall into."

Quentin Hyder confirms that "the hard-ball player has a hard time getting out of his system the power game of driving the ball low on the front wall and trying to hit it past his opponent. If you're going to mess around playing the hard-ball shots, your opponent, if he's stronger or younger, is going to kill you by just outdriving you." Quentin's game is built on lobs and drops, with which he often beats younger, stronger opponents.

In coaching his players, Bob Callahan observes, "One of the key changes that hard-ballers have to make is an attitude adjustment, that when you hit your drop shots and your boasts you're not going for the half-inch-over-the-tin winner. If you do, you are too aggressive and will make mistakes. In soft ball, you do not see as many outright winners. You don't see a ball roll out and a guy just not get there. You see a lot more pressure balls force the guy to make errors, where he's just so run around that he barely gets his racquet up and just can't get it back."

"With soft ball, it's not any one shot," says Frank Satterthwaite. "It's the effect of hitting with great accuracy and continually putting pressure on your opponent in many little ways, so that eventually there's a breakdown, either physical or mental or both. It's not as though you make a dramatic shot. Soft ball is the accumulation of small advantages, building the pressure, and then the breakdown."

Jay Nelson believes that "the emotional, attitudinal makeup in hard-ball and soft-ball players is very different. If you are at the T in hard ball, you have to be a little hyper, a little nervous, you have to be prepared on almost any exchange that your opponent may hit a winner. Second, you have to be prepared to dash, to fly, to really move. If he hits a good shot you have to stretch out hard. I'm talking even when the guy's deep and you have pretty decent position, because there's always the three-wall nick, or a straight drop from deep, or a hard, low cross-court—boom!—for the winner.

"In soft ball, you can relax in the sense that if you hit a good deep shot, you're probably not going to lose to an outright winner. That's not a bad feeling—just the whole attitude during the game is more relaxed. There's more striding going on rather than panicky dashing. If you've got that panicky or hard-edged nervousness at the T, it's going to cost you. You just can't afford to be pumped and psyched in soft ball."

Attitudes on court are the main determinant of playing style. Paul Assaiante watched two opposite styles confront each other when Mark Talbott and Michael Desaulniers, both top hard-ballers, played soft ball together: "Mark came in and exposed the weaknesses in Michael's style by playing a very slowed down, rope-a-dope type of game. Michael played a frenetic style that can never be transferred to the soft-ball game. He just got disrobed because he wanted to play such an up-tempo."

Mark himself has this to say about his style: "I think my game, my style, has been adaptable to soft ball. I've always been able to hit the ball to good length and I do that well with a soft ball. I hit the ball high and keep it going. I'm patient out there, don't make a lot of mistakes, get a lot of balls back, run well, so that all relates pretty well to soft ball."

HOW STYLE TRANSLATES INTO TACTICS

As the hard-baller adjusts to hitting shots that move his opponent around instead of going for winners, he is rewarded with the pleasure of controlling the flow of a rally. Jay Nelson describes this vividly: "In soft ball, you can get the guy on a string, you know, basically bust his chops, just work the guy something fierce. That's kind of satisfying—finally you have him desperate and he stays off balance, always scurrying to get your next shot. I guess it's the fact that it's not so slam-bam. It gives the appearance of being more cerebral, don't you think?"

Emily Goodfellow echoes this thought: "You can't just be a great physical specimen and go out to grind your opponent down. You have to have a real game plan, much more so than in hard ball. When you got desperate, you'd whale on the hard ball and hit a three-wall and hope for the nick—it was a more reactive kind of game. Whereas in soft ball there are times when I see players really trying to work through something during the course of the point. 'Uh oh, how am I going to get out of here, I'm in pretty good shape so I can keep the point going, but I'm not going to win the point that way. I've gotta start putting pressure on my opponent.' Because the pace is slower, it promotes a lot more gray matter being put to work."

A direct result of the slower ball is the greater number of opportunities to move the ball short in the court. In soft ball at the top levels, there are a much higher percentage of drops and boasts, and a lot more re-dropping.

Demer Holleran describes how the purpose of the boast changes in soft ball: "We need to think of the boast as a moving shot more than as a finishing shot. We used to hit a three-wall boast mostly to win the point, particularly for women, who used the three-wall as a precision shot. So it's harder for us to hit a boast with a lot more margin just to move an opponent and tire her out, get her off balance. That still doesn't come naturally to me."

Gary Waite, the top-ranked North American professional soft-ball player, teaches youngsters how to adjust to a soft-ball style. "You need to get the kid on the court and play rallies where he doesn't get to hit any winners, where he's on the end of the rally. You need to instill in the kid the mentality of being able to create an offensive position out of a defensive position through a two- or three-shot pattern, not immediately."

Frank Satterthwaite says that when he switches from hard

ball to soft ball he mentally flips the court: "In hard ball, you take your opponent deep, then you take him short, often winning on a three-wall nick or a drop. In soft ball, you take your opponent deep, then take him short in order ultimately to beat him deep. The only sure putaway in soft ball is when you have your opponent short and then smack the ball deep without touching the side wall—that ball's unretrievable."

In summarizing what tactics a soft-ball newcomer must develop, Bob Callahan observes: "There are three important skills you need to acquire as soon as you can: being able to cut the ball off to maintain court position, moving someone forward and then following up, and how to play defensively from the back corner. Hard-ball players don't take advantage of these skills. They don't cut the ball off enough and they don't use the straight drops, the boasts, and then follow up as well as they should. And defensively, it's not very often in hard ball that a ball doesn't come out enough that you can't drive it again, so you have to learn about defensive boasting."

Brett Martin (Australia) and Rodney Martin (Australia).

4. SOFT-BALL FUNDAMENTALS

The hard-ballers—me among them—were wrong when they thought that soft ball is mainly a game of calisthenics and attrition with little emphasis on technique. And we were baffled that Americans rarely got past the opening rounds of international tournaments, yet the soft-ballers would come over here and, after a short period of adjustment to the hard ball, beat most of our best players.

The excuse often given was that soft-ballers were "training animals" and naturally superior in the much longer points typical of their game. This simplification obscured the fact that soft ball is a game that places a huge premium on correct technique, precision stroking, and agile movement. To win at soft ball, a player must master these techniques, starting with the most basic of fundamentals, the grip.

THE GRIP

My first squash coach used to quote one of the great French masters of the foil, who said he held his instrument like "un petit oiseau"—firmly enough so it couldn't fly away but gently so he wouldn't crush it. The lesson my coach conveyed was how important it is to begin the point with a firm but relaxed connection between you and your racquet. I also learned later that you cannot begin the stroke if your muscles are already tensed: you first have to cancel out the tension.

Squash is a game of precision, where feel and touch are critical. "If your racquet's not sharp," observes Gary Waite, "it doesn't matter how fit you are. You're not going to win." The grip that delivers the best feel and touch is the continental grip—the same as used in hard ball—because it provides more contact with the fingers than with the palm of the hand. In fact, there should be a little air between the handle and your palm when you are in the ready position.

David Pearson, British coach of many world-class players, stresses in his teaching of the grip that you control and guide the racquet with the thumb, forefinger, and wrist, while using the other three fingers in a more relaxed manner to stabilize everything. "There's a lot of freedom in soft ball," he says, and this grip with its looseness helps achieve the characteristic flowing swing.

Many coaches teach the continental grip with the "handshake" method: hold the racquet shank in your left hand, reach out with your right and shake hands with the handle. This concept emphasizes the extension of the forefinger and the curling of the other three fingers, with the thumb and forefinger forming a "V" at the top. The left top edge of the racquet shank should intersect the point of the "V." The forefinger is separated from the others and wraps around the shank as if gripping a trigger. The thumb fits nicely into the gap between the forefinger and middle finger.

Jahangir Khan makes a slight modification to this grip which has been adopted by many of the world's top players. He rotates the racquet about one-eighth of a turn in a clockwise direction, opening the face and just exposing the leading edge of the shank when viewed from the top.

With this grip, you get slightly more undercut on the forehand and greater control on the backhand and on volleys. The grip is the same for both forehand and backhand.

Think of your grip as the place where your orders get carried out, where your energy is focused. Your fingers become so

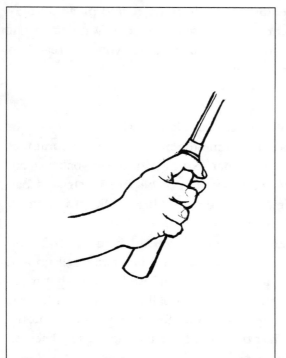

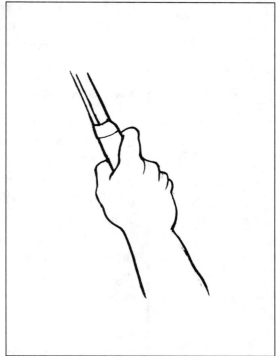

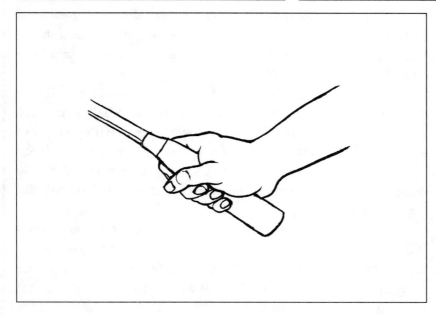

The Grip.
From back (upper left), note the extended forefinger with thumb fitting between first two fingers. From front (left), three fingers wrap around with the thumb resting on top of the middle finger. From top (upper right), the thumb and forefinger form a "V" and the leading edge of the racquet shaft is barely visible when viewed from the top.

SOFT-BALL FUNDAMENTALS

sensitized after the requisite time in practice and play that they convey your intent and energize your racquet. With the right connection between you and your racquet, you are ready to swing with comfort and control.

THE STROKE

In speaking of the soft-ball stroke, Ned Edwards says, "One of the things that has stayed with me the most has been a comment from Chris Dittmar [a former No. 1 world soft-baller from Australia] about how important it is to be able to strike a ball properly. When he came over and played hard ball, I was amazed at his facility with the racquet.

"A lot of us, when we faced the transition to the soft ball, thought, 'God, now all we're going to do is hit the ball up and down the rail and run, and run, and run.' And I think that misses the point. If Americans think of soft ball as a contest of fitness, we will continue to be cannon fodder for the good international players, because we'll just be sending the ball right back, keeping it in play as they carve us up."

Striking the ball well in soft ball is very different from hard ball. In soft-ball squash you need a *big* swing, more like in baseball or golf than tennis. You start high and end high. Some have described it as a big "U."

It is the nature of the ball and the need for speed that determines the size of the stroke. With the lively hard ball, you could reach out and from just the elbow down or even with your hand still flick the ball effectively and keep yourself in the rally. Even with a short, compact swing, the ball—because it would hardly compress at all—leaped off the strings to its target. The ball did the work for you.

The soft ball is a *soft* ball. Its far greater elasticity and equal lack of ability to spring back means that the more it compresses, the more it loses speed. There is in fact a shot among the elite players where they hit the ball with such great force that it virtually flattens against the front wall and hardly comes off at all—a "stun drive" they call it.

Satinder Bajwa, North American business manager for Jansher

Khan and a top player in the 30's age-bracket, gave his engineer's analysis of this phenomenon. "The soft ball is so soft that if you hit it too hard you have a reverse effect. It just stops. You can get beyond elasticity. You never see Jansher slamming at the ball, and yet he hits the ball as hard as anybody when he wants to. What he really does is get optimum strength ratio with the elasticity of the ball. You've gotta caress that ball, you've gotta love it."

Due to its greater compressibility, the soft ball squashes into your strings and sits on them longer—it actually feels heavier than the hard ball. And thus it takes far more head speed in the stroke to generate the desired speed of flight in the ball.

Fortunately, it is not necessary to use brute force to get head speed, you can let the momentum of the swing do most of the work for you. Simply by taking a big enough backswing—getting the arm and the racquet high enough—you get a lot of "free" power from gravity as the racquet comes down through the stroke.

David Pearson, when demonstrating the correct stroke, points out the need to have lots of room between the racquet head and the body as you take the racquet back. On his backhand, for example, he first pushes the racquet head on a horizontal diagonal away from his hip towards the left rear corner, and then raises it on a vertical diagonal back over his left shoulder, well away from his head. "From there," he says, "you let go and throw from the shoulder. Your elbow locks out about a foot before impact and this locking gives you the power."

There is a third phase to the backswing used by some of the advanced players where they continue to take the racquet back until the head is pointing at the front wall, in theory to give the racquet a longer travel path and more speed before impact with the ball. David does not recommend this, particularly for players trying to convert from a hard-ball stroke, or simply learning a proper soft-ball swing from scratch.

The experience of Goldie Edwards is poignant and useful for a hard-ball player trying to convert to the soft-ball stroke: "Initially, when I started trying to hit that soft ball, I really had a wrist problem and even an elbow problem for a while because I tried to use my wrist. You have to use the whole arm, and that is so foreign when you've been playing hard ball. That changes your timing, and with all the extra effort I would get puffed out. I would be huffing from just hitting the ball in the warmup, trying to move it, because my strokes were so inefficient. So I had to learn how to hit the ball correctly. The stroke is so much bigger, you have to get the racquet way up and the arm up, then bring the arm and the racquet and everything down and hit the ball squarely. It just takes practice."

Demer Holleran had a similar and equally instructive experience in relearning her stroke: "Changing my swing was a really big issue. I ran into a lot of problems with tennis elbow because I was playing the ball too close to my body and trying to muscle the ball instead of letting the racquet do the work and using my upper body more in the stroke. Still to this day, I'm always told by my coach to stay away from the ball, stretch to the ball."

There is a principle of physics behind the need to keep the ball away from your body—it contributes directly to increased centrifugal power at the end of a longer arc (swing).

Bob Callahan describes the need to convert one of the Princeton freshmen from the typical hard-ball stroke: "He's got nice racquet skills, a pretty compact swing, quite a short backswing, and when he's converting to soft ball, he's going to have to lengthen his entire swing. He's got to sweep through the ball rather than punching everything."

Goldie sums up nicely the important criteria for the soft-ball stroke: "You just have to buy into the fact that you have to develop a bigger swing that uses the large muscles of the shoulder. And you have to get your weight into it. You could get away with so much in hard ball because it was so reflexive, you reacted to the ball. With soft ball, you really have to *work* the ball, you have to make it happen."

And Demer, too: "In soft ball you need more shoulder turn and a bigger follow-through. And really just the concept of being loose, holding the racquet a bit looser, loosening your whole arm and torso, and turning from the waist. All those things, I think. It's a bigger, smoother, more natural swing, more like swinging a baseball bat I would say."

The Forehand Drive.
Start the stroke high
with upper arm parallel
to floor, bent elbow,
hand and racquet high.
Take a smooth, long
stroke, following
through in the direction
of the target. The stroke
ends high, also with
bent elbow.

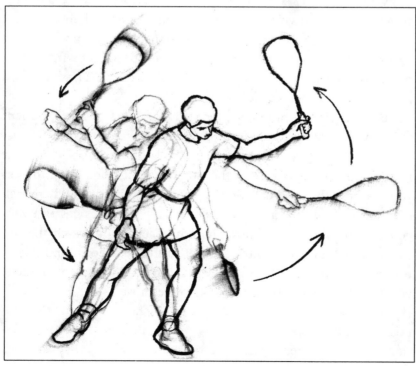

The Backhand Drive.
High racquet as in
forehand but with
elbow pointed slightly
downward. Take care
to follow through in
upwards direction to
avoid hitting opponent
with racquet.

**SOFT-BALL
FUNDAMENTALS**

POSITION AND THE GOOD FOOTWORK

"Position is important," says Mark Talbott. "The court is so big and the ball so slow that you need maximum preparation to power the ball. If you're really stretched out up front, you can't power the ball to the back of the court, where in hard ball you could flick your wrist and smack it to the back of the court. In soft ball you really need to get up there early, and work hard with your feet to be in position to have a variety of shots as options."

Goldie Edwards agrees: "With hard ball, one of the things that made it so much easier was that the ball came to you. The soft ball doesn't do that. You actually have to go and get the ball. So that takes movement, let alone the fact that it's a bigger court."

Get on the T! That's the admonition and that's the position we all want to be in when waiting for our opponent to hit the ball. However, it rarely means you should literally stand on the intersection of the half-court and short lines. The ideal T position "moves around" depending on where the ball is, how well it was hit, and where your opponent is standing.

When the rally is even, you should stand straddling the half-court line about two feet behind the short line. When you have the offensive, it's better to be a little farther forward. If your opponent can hit either short or long, you need to be more prepared for the short shot because it's over quicker. There is more time to go back and retrieve a deep shot.

In general, you should be prepared mentally for your opponent to hit every shot up to the front of the court, with your weight distribution forward, balanced over the balls of your feet—"on your toes" as they say. Because of the slower ball, it's not going to pass you as fast as the hard ball. So you should expect to cut off any ball laterally or be able to go forward for it. And if it does get past you, you can move back at a nice smooth pace. If you watch the top soft-ball players, they almost saunter to the back court and take it off the back wall. The move sideways to the volley is a quick move and the move to the front is an explosive move.

There are two moments in the rally when you want to be in position and stopped—the *waiting* position and the *shooting* position. At both moments you want to be poised and evenly balanced.

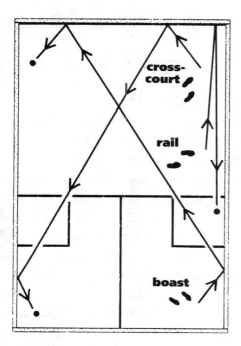

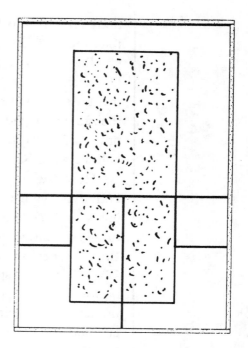

Fig. 3. Position for the Feet. At rear, point feet into back corner for hitting boasts. At mid-court, point feet straight at side wall to hit rails and other straight shots. At front, point feet into front corner to hit cross-courts.

Fig. 4. "Stay on the Carpet." Most players should be able to hit the ball correctly by keeping at least one foot in the center, shaded area of the court. Playing within this smaller rectangle saves energy and promotes a fully extended soft-ball-style stroke.

We have discussed the waiting position, now let's look at the shooting position—remembering that cardinal squash principle of wanting your front shoulder pointing at the target. Translated to foot positions (Figure 3), this means you should point your feet into the side wall for straight shots, towards the rear corner for boasts, and towards the front corner for cross-courts.

The orthodox shooting position for forehand rails is often violated in match play, especially among the top players, for very good reasons: you can move more quickly without having to make a full turn and reach farther to the shot by stretching out with the right ("wrong") foot forward and then push off more readily to get back to the T. This more open stance makes it as easy to hit a cross-court shot as to hit a rail. When making this unorthodox move, you just want to be sure to get your upper body around into the backswing, which requires more twisting than the orthodox stance.

The concept of the "unit turn," taught at Princeton University's squash camp, is a blending of stroking and movement. As you move to shooting position, turn your upper body at the same time you take your racquet back. This gets you ready in one fluid move that then uncoils all together as you strike the ball. Jahangir Khan "swivels" his body into the shot.

How you move is a very personal matter determined by your body type, your training, and even your psyche. Ian McKenzie, in his book *The Squash Workshop*, captures these differences beautifully: "Hunt, who strode the court rhythmically and won eight British Open titles, was the athlete. Zaman was the dancer. Jahangir, the cat, sprung with a speed and unleashed a power that no other player could live with. Jansher fluctuates between unmatchable bursts of speed, a seemingly instantaneous recovery, and a languid relaxation that flashes into action."

The good news, even though "you actually have to go and get the ball," is that you don't have to travel as far as you might think on the bigger court. Remember that you need to keep the ball away from you to get full power in your stroke; therefore, even with those glued-to-the-wall shots, you don't need to step beyond a point from which you can reach the wall with an extended racquet. This cuts the court down to a rectangle of *less than half* the total court area (Figure 4). Paul Assaiante calls this the "carpet" and keeps reminding players during lessons to "stay on the carpet." It may be hard to accept, but most players can reach shots up front in three strides, shots in the back corners in two strides, and anything sideways in one.

David Pearson has a very clear presentation of the movement patterns and why they are so critical to a proper soft-ball game, which I have interpreted in the accompanying diagram (Figure 5). You wish to move from position A to position B to strike the ball at point C. Some players will take a path of direct interception with the ball, which is the worst choice, causing a jammed-against-the-body shot with little power and less control.

Other players, understanding the correct position and stance relative to the point of impact, will go directly to that position, which works okay for hard ball but denies the essential nature of the soft-ball stroke—hitting the ball from a stretched-out position with a fully extended racquet.

Therefore, the correct path to the ball is along an arc (Figure 6) that actually forces you to hit from a stretched-out stance. As David puts it, "If the approach is correct, the swing works very naturally—it's what makes a soft-ball player look like a soft-ball player." Moving along this arc, you take one last lunging step—it puts you into the stretched-out stance, keeps the rear foot on the carpet, and makes for a shorter distance when pushing off back to the T.

To master the right patterns of movement and learn correct footwork, there is one best exercise, known as "ghosting," where you go onto the court by yourself with a racquet and no ball. You play imaginary shots, moving from the T to the shooting position, preparing for the shot, stroking and recovering to the T.

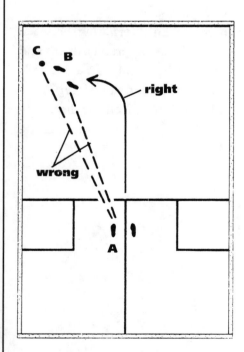

Fig. 5. Choose the Right Path.

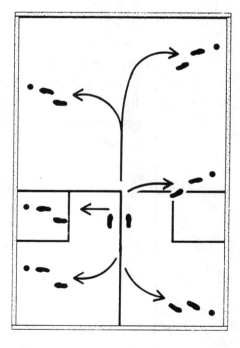

Fig. 6. Move Along an Arc.

Initially, if you are just learning the footwork or trying to break a bad overstriding habit, work out the steps as in a first dance lesson and move through them slowly until your familiarity grows and you can speed them up. Concentrate on arriving in position on the correct foot, executing the stroke properly and pushing off immediately to the T. Do this in all directions—go to the front, hit a drop, return, intercept a cross-court and volley, return, go to the rear and boast, return. Hit serves and move fluidly to the T. Gradually you will drive these moves into your muscle memory and use them automatically in your matches. But keep doing this exercise periodically; even the very best players continually do ghosting to keep their footwork sharp.

Ghosting can be taken one level higher by working out sequences of shots that occur during a match and playing an imaginary opponent. You hit your shot, recover and wait for your "opponent" to hit his, move and hit yours, and so on. This gamelike ghosting is similar to the *kata* exercise in karate, where emphasis is placed on developing perfect form and mental focus while fighting imaginary opponents.

Jay Nelson discovered when he began alternating between soft ball and hard ball that the greater focus on preparedness and stroking in soft ball was a big asset in his hard-ball game. He calls it "the training wheel phenomenon" because it slows everything down. "I found going back to soft ball reintroduced the discipline and gave me the time to do the good footwork, and you must do the good footwork."

Cassie Jackman (England) and Suzanne Horner (England).

5. THE SIX BASIC SHOTS

There are six basic shots in soft-ball squash—the *rail* (straight drive), *cross-court, boast, lob, drop,* and *kill.* All others are either variations, strokes, odd shots, or shot situations. The *high lob* and the *semi lob* are variations. The *drive* (ground stroke) and the *volley* are strokes. The *serve* and the *return* are shot situations. The *reverse corner* and the *three-wall nick,* favorites of hard-ball players, are odd shots in soft ball, particularly on the wide court.

Let's analyze each basic shot, consider its fine points, and look at how to practice it. By following these instructions and drills, and by practicing regularly, you will learn how to hit these shots consistently in a match.

THE RAIL

The most used and useful shot in squash is the *rail.* It is hit to run within inches of the side wall all the way back into the corner, forcing your opponent at best to hit a nonthreatening, or even a very weak, return.

"Driving to a length" is the phrase soft-ballers use to describe both rails and cross-courts hit deeply into the rear corners. Hard-

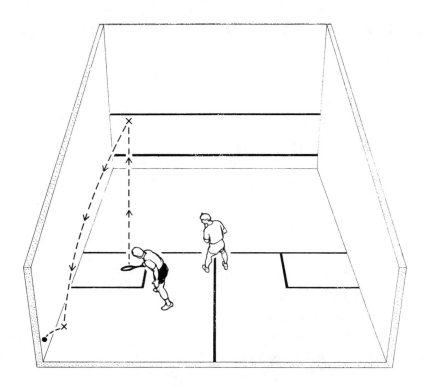

Rail. The ball is struck just behind the point in your swing where your racquet would form a right angle with the wall in order to produce a rebound that gradually closes with the side wall as the ball moves to the rear corner. Target height on the front wall changes depending on where you are in the court, how hard you hit, and the temperature of the ball—always hitting high enough to reach the back wall before the second bounce.

ballers too are grooved on hitting deep balls. The catch is that length in soft ball is a totally different concept. "I think a good definition of length in soft ball is 'one bounce, back wall,'" Bob Callahan says, "where in hard ball, great length is 'bounce-and-die' just short of the back wall.

The reasons for this difference—and for most differences in the two games—are the speed and bounce of the ball. The soft ball—traveling much slower and angling off more sharply after each bounce—is too easy to cut off if it doesn't bounce well behind the service box and hit the back wall before the second bounce. The ball hardly comes off the back even when it hits rather high, so it's better to overhit than to underhit.

To get proper length you must have proper height on the front wall. In fact, height, not pace, is the main determinant of length in soft ball. This simple difference, so clear and oft-stated to converting hard-ballers, is nevertheless a daunting obstacle. Hard-ballers are accustomed to calibrating their front-wall tar-

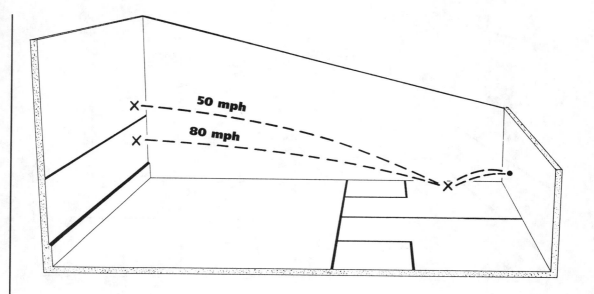

gets for rail shots in inches-above-the-tin; soft-ballers calibrate their drives from the cut line—a full four-plus feet higher on the front wall. "So you have to rearrange your mind set to see that the ball hits high enough on the front wall," says Demer Holleran. "And to see that can take a few years. You can say it to yourself as much as you want, but it won't happen until you have hit enough rails with the soft ball to groove it into your shot reflexes."

A "pure" rail, in addition to having the correct depth, comes ever closer without quite touching the side wall, or if it does, it touches well behind the service box. Because the soft ball moves slower, you have to be so much more exact in terms of tightness to the wall—the perfect rail travels so tight to the wall that it seems to be rolling along its surface. You may be able to power the ball deep, but if it's a foot off the wall, you're asking for trouble; in hard ball, the rail shot went so fast that your opponent was challenged by its speed and length alone.

THE CROSS-COURT

The *cross-court* shot wide-court in soft ball is far more important than in hard ball because it takes advantage of the extra 2 1/2 feet

The 50-mph Rail. At mid-levels of play, and even at the top levels when long rallies are being played, it is useful to hit a slower ball aimed higher on the front wall in order to get the depth required of any good rail shot. You have more control, and if that means you can hit a shot that runs consistently tighter to the wall, then you should hit the "50-mph rail shot" rather than a fast ball that bounces short or wide of the wall.

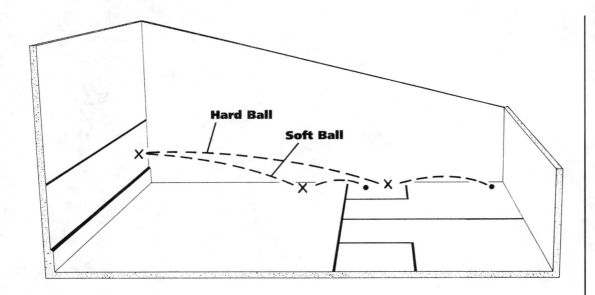

Hard Ball

Soft Ball

of court width (see page 101, Soft Ball on the Narrow Court). It is the second choice after a rail for sending your opponent into the back corners of the court. The cross-court is an easy trap to fall into when choosing which shot to hit because it is a more natural shot to hit when facing forward. However, when hit at the right time, it can be just as effective as a deep, tight rail.

When to hit a cross-court instead of a rail depends on how well you can control the two shots and on where your opponent is standing. If he is balanced on the T, he has a good chance of cutting off your cross-court and volleying it into the front corner (against a good volleyer you would obviously hit fewer cross-courts). On the other hand, if he thinks you're going to hit another rail shot and leans in that direction, that is a good time to cross-court him.

Aim the ball to hit the side wall slightly *past* the point opposite where he is standing—exactly opposite gives him the chance to back up and take it off the wall. As we have said, the soft ball is such a gritty ball, it angles back into the court rather than running along the wall, so the extra depth before hitting the wall is crucial.

Jay Nelson finds that he has his greatest success in soft ball when he hits deep cross-courts. "For the hard-baller coming to

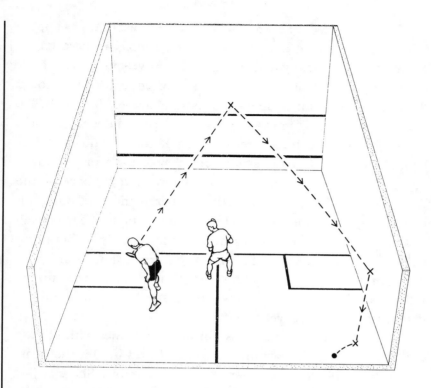

Cross-Court. The ball is struck well in front of the body with racquet face tilted back to get good height. The target on the side wall is about three feet above the floor and behind your opponent, forcing him into a deeper retrieve. The swing crosses in front of the body, making the cross-court a more natural shot to play when facing the front wall, which we usually do when moving forward in the court.

soft ball, this is perhaps the biggest surprise—that you can hit a good, high cross-court with a cool, flowing stroke, and the ball will sometimes do funny things, like 'smother' in the back corner. The hard-baller thinks, 'If I hit cross-court, four feet up on the wall, it's going to tee up off the back wall and a lot of bad things can happen to me.' I know at the soft-ball Nationals this past October I was geared up for the cross-court and it was very effective. I have to keep reminding myself to think that way because, for a hard-baller, it's counterintuitive."

THE BOAST

More than any other shot, the *boast* earns for squash its reputation as a game of angles. It is also the shot that varies most between the soft-ball and hard-ball games. Thus, the player who learns early on to distinguish and use the very different boasts of the soft-ball game will become a true soft-ball player that much quicker than his peers.

A major difference in soft ball is that the boast is just as important defensively as it is offensively. For example, in hard ball it wasn't very often that you had to play defensively in the very back of the court; the ball usually came out far enough so you could drive it again or hit a three-wall nick. However, in soft ball a defensive boast is often the only way to retrieve a deeply hit ball.

When you are forced into the back corner and can't get behind the ball for a full swing—no chance for a rail or cross-court—your safest, easiest shot to buy time and get back on the T is a *standard defensive boast*. It is hit into the side wall with medium pace and lots of lift so that it "loops" up to the front wall well above the tin and angles over to the other wall, bouncing twice before it gets there. This is not a forcing shot. Your opponent can usually reach it and hit a drop shot, making you run the full diagonal to stay in the rally. The lesson here is to avoid the defensive boast whenever you can.

Demer Holleran found this out in her matches with the top British and Australian women players. "I find if I hit the boast out of the back corners, I get in a lot of trouble. She can just drop. I would rather use the boast as a shot to hurt her after she's hit a weak rail, where I'm in front—then it makes a lot more sense. They're likely to get it at the top levels, but at least I've worked them and hurt them."

A more advanced defensive boast out of the back corners is the *skid boast*. It is hit hard, high, and farther forward onto the side wall, then strikes the front wall near the top and arcs back across court in the manner of a cross-court lob. It is something of a novelty shot and when used sparingly, especially below the top level of play, it can throw off your opponent and maybe even win the point. It's a little harder to hit on the backhand because you don't have the same leverage.

Mark Talbott says about the skid boast, "I use it occasionally, though not very much against a better player because it tends to produce a loose cross-court lob. I think you can get away with it on an amateur level because they don't volley quite as much. It's hard to be accurate with it, you have to be a good player to hit it."

There is yet a third defensive boast which should only be hit

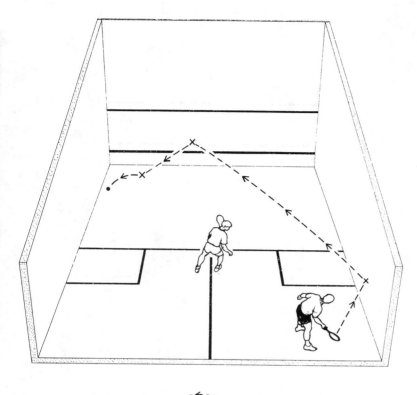

Back-Corner Defensive Boast.

Point toes into corner, crouch slightly to get under the ball. Take ball behind where you would for a rail, hitting upwards with a medium-paced stroke and very open racquet face. The ball should be hit into the side wall at about a 45 degree angle and "float" to a point just left of center on the front wall, well above the tin, then angle widely and die before hitting the other side.

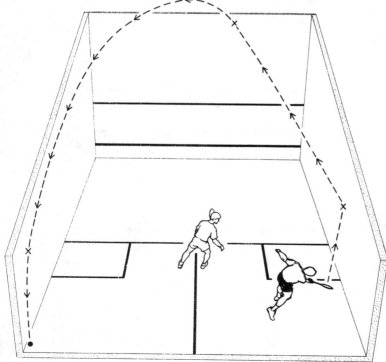

Skid Boast.

Hit as a surprise from the same position and stance as a back-corner defensive boast. Strike the ball hard, with a very open face. The target is much higher and nearer the front—about opposite the short line, up about six feet on the side wall. The ball angles to a point high up on the front wall and rebounds like a cross-court lob, hits the other side wall near the rear of the service box, bounces, and dies in the corner.

Working Boast. Use this shot when you get a short, straight ball and your opponent is behind you. Shape for a rail, let the ball pass behind you, hit upwards with open-faced, short swing. The ball angles sharply into the side, travels to the front wall a few inches above the tin and carries across the front of the court, bouncing twice before hitting the opposite side.

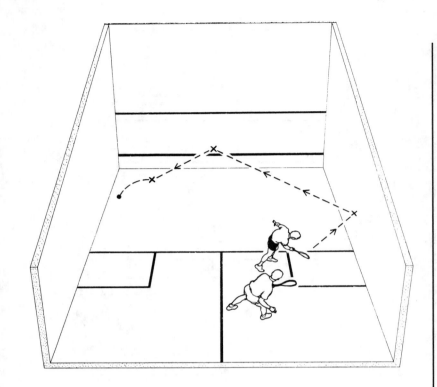

Trickle Boast. A deception shot, hit when you get a short ball near the side wall and your opponent is expecting a straight ball (rail or drop). Show him the rail prepara- tion, then turn racquet face into the wall at the last minute, hit gently upwards with open face at a very sharp angle so the ball comes off the front wall at a wide angle.

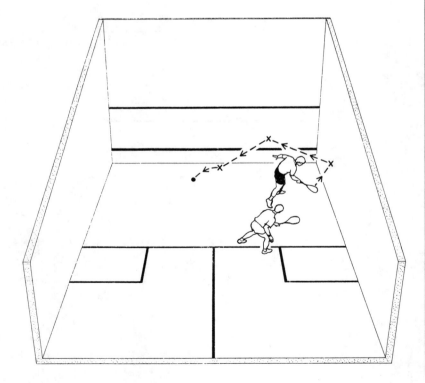

as a last resort—the *back-wall boast.* When you have been passed by a ball that is going to die in the rear of the court, hit the ball upwards onto the back wall, aiming if possible to produce a high, cross-court lob that drops and dies in the opposite front corner. Very few players practice this, hitting instead a parallel ball that gets eaten up on the next shot.

Twenty years ago, when North Americans were just starting to play soft ball, we ran into the unfamiliar *working boast,* a shot that left us puzzled not only as to its use on our narrow courts but also its meaning. Peter Briggs, one of the Americans then starting to play soft ball, says, "All it really means is that if you hit it correctly, the guy just has to bust his butt chasing after it. The English game is centered around making the guy work, exposing whether he's in good shape or not. And with this shot, you get exposed in a hurry."

The offensive, working boast is not intended to win the point but to work your opponent by moving him to the front of the court. This is a shot that should be acquired as early as possible by players at all levels. It is the easiest first shot to learn for hitting short—much easier than a drop. The boast can be hit with a lot more pace than the drop and aimed comfortably above the tin, with a much lower risk.

THE LOB

Quentin Hyder loves to lob. So does Goldie Edwards, who says, "You can mess up a lot of people by putting the ball high to the back, and stay in with younger players who don't know how to handle that, which most of the less experienced players don't." The fundamental game Quentin was taught from the age of thirteen is a lob-and-drop game. "The aim is to play soft, high lobs, get the guy behind you, and then play the short shot."

To a hard-ball player, hyped on power and speed, the *lob* is a rarely used, even wimpy shot. If you overhit it slightly, it comes back out on the court, giving your opponent a fat put-away ball. But in soft ball, you can hit the lob with a wider range of force and get a trajectory that works. Indeed, the lob is a major weapon—to defend and to attack. Yet, paradoxically, even for the

Cross-Court Lob— From Front. Ideally, you have reached the front with a high enough backswing to threaten a rail, with the option also to hit a drop or a lob. On the forehand, this would involve an open, stretched-out stance. Stroke softly well under the ball with a very open face, with a pronounced upwards lift, hit the ball high onto the front wall, angled back to the opposite corner. It should strike the other side wall a foot or two below the out line and bounce tight in the corner before hitting rear wall.

Cross-Court Lob— From Rear. This is a defensive shot when hit from the rear of the court. It slows the game down and gives you a chance to get back on the T.

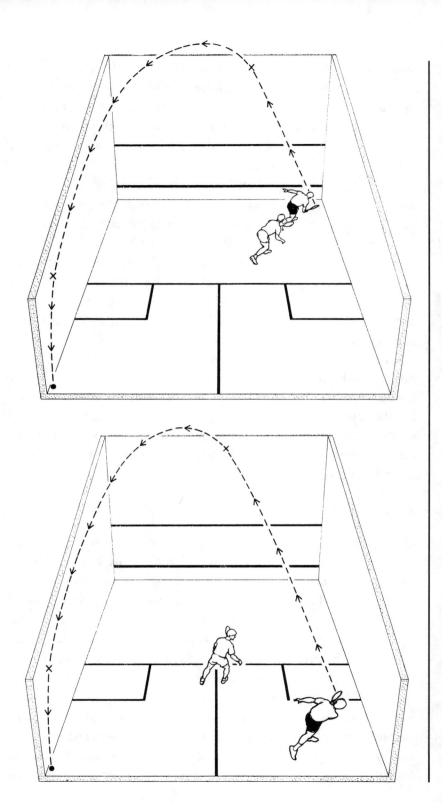

native soft-baller, the lob is an underrated, underused shot.

Why is the lob such a valuable shot? Because it buys time when you're under pressure, enabling you to regain the T and go onto the offensive. It slows the game down when you're tired. It takes advantage of an opponent who cannot volley well. And if it's hit just right, it can be a winner, falling almost vertically to die in the back corners. As Frank Satterthwaite observes, "It's a soft, mushy little ball, but if it's dropping from the rafters, it's whipping past you by the time it gets down there, and it's damn hard to turn a ball say 60 degrees from its path with any accuracy."

The lob can be hit defensively from the back of the court to slow the pace of the game. It is far more threatening, however, when you are up front, your opponent comes up with you, and then you send a slow skyball up over his head to the opposite rear corner.

Jay Nelson describes his use of the lob: "I know from my own experience there are far more winners hit in the wide courts using cross-court lobs than in narrow-court soft ball. The very top players do a lot of cross-court lobbing. Basically, what you do is you're showing the guy a drop or maybe a rail, he's got to be up there leaning, and you flick it high and across court. He's running back and the ball's coming down deep in the corner. You get a lot of winners."

THE DROP

"Man does not live by depth alone," intoned Bob Callahan at the Princeton University squash camp as we were preparing to take up the fine points of the short game. Clearly, it is the short game in soft-ball squash that often finishes the point. And of all the short shots, the one used to attack and score most often among the better players is the *drop shot*.

The challenge of the drop shot is to earn the right to use it. First you need to master an advanced shot, and then you must wait for the right moment to hit it. It is better to learn the *straight drop* before the *cross drop*. "If you look at the pros playing," says Neil Pomphrey, an English player now ranked among the top 35-age-group players in the U.S., "they play very few cross-court drops. Almost everything is a straight drop with the aim of leaving it as tight with the side wall as they can. If it's tight enough, the only shot your opponent can hit is a redrop."

The straight drop is difficult because there is very little margin for error—if it's too low, you tin, if it's too high or too far out in the court, you tee the ball up for your opponent. You should hit the straight drop to make sure it catches the side wall before hitting the floor, which will further slow its pace and produce a nick effect.

There is a big difference in stroke preparation for a drop shot between hard ball and soft ball, as explained by Frank Satterthwaite: "In soft ball, if you hold your racquet low when you're up front, your opponent knows that you cannot gun it and he will tiptoe right up behind you and be in position to put your short shot away. This is arguably the hardest habit to break for an advanced player."

Demer Holleran spent a lot of time working on this, and only in the past year has she developed the ability to hit the ball hard from the front when she's very stretched out. "If you're really under pressure and not as good technically, you tend to redrop or lob," she said. "But it's great to have the variety and be able to hit the ball hard from up there, too. You have to be on the ball faster in order to take that full swing."

The right moment for a drop shot should be the concurrence of a rather easy ball and an opponent who is out of position, either off the T or behind you. The drop is the classic response to a back-corner defensive boast or to a short cross-court. However, the drop carries with it the obligation to get yourself back and to the side so your opponent can get to it; otherwise, you invite a let or the award of a stroke.

As for the cross-court drop, I was discussing with Emily Goodfellow how hard it was for me as an ex-hard-baller to learn to hit the ball so that it catches the side wall.

Emily: "I can't hit it to save my life."

Austin: "There's a repetitive drill I saw an Indian player using at the club that you can use to learn that shot."

Emily: "Forget it, Austin. You're dreaming."

Maybe so, but if I keep hitting it . . .

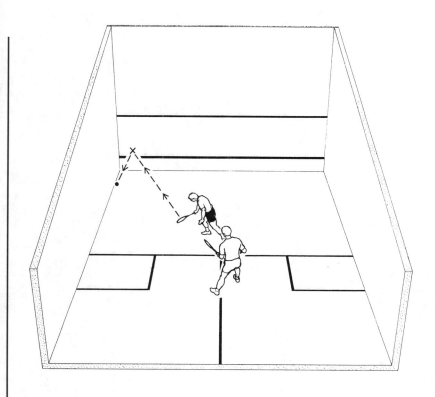

Straight Drop. Go in with good balance and a high racquet, as for a rail. Bend down to the level of the ball, use a shorter, firm swing, and follow through to guide the ball to its target. Angle the shot in to catch the side wall just above the floor. To get the ball to die as soon as possible, hit with a very open face and underspin.

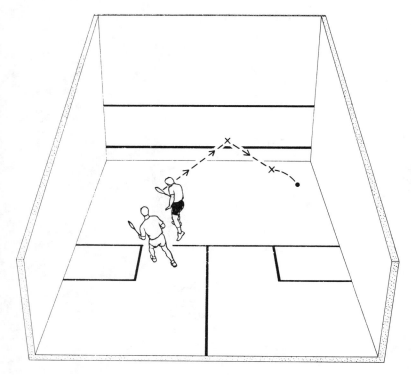

Cross-Court Drop. This shot is a good alternative if your opponent has committed to one side of the court, expecting you to hit a drop or a rail. The ball can be angled very wide on the front wall to move in the direction opposite to which he is leaning.

The Forehand Straight Kill. Stance is open and more erect than for a forehand drive, the backswing shorter, the volley stroke sliced downwards with shorter follow-through. The ball is aimed to hit the front wall inches above the tin and die in the nick.

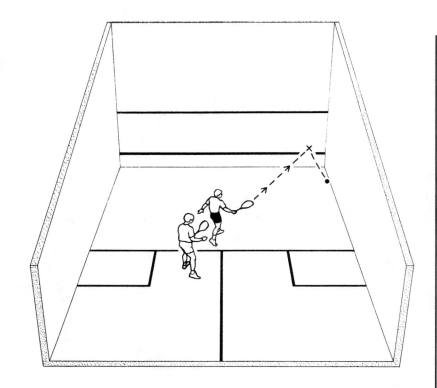

The Volley Cross-Court Nick. Usually hit from near the T, the stroke is across the body and downwards, relying on the sharp angle down and across to produce a higher probability of a nick.

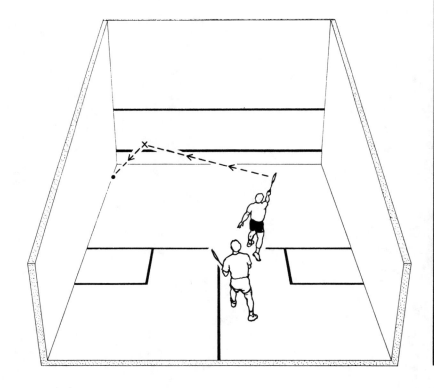

THE KILL

I watched Brett Martin, the No. 2 soft-ball player in the world, step into a loose, waist-high ball short of the T, cock an abbreviated forehand backswing, and bang the ball hard into the right front corner just over the tin for a winner. It was a *kill* or "stun drive," which with its cross-court variant are the slam dunks of squash.

Afterwards, Brett described the shot in the offhand manner of natural athletes who can't fully appreciate the rarity of their talents. "That's just a basic forehand kill," he said. "You slice the ball from as high as you can to get it down off the front wall as quick as you can into the nick. If you hit it flat, it's going to come farther back, so you slice it to get the ball to hit the front wall and go down."

The straight and cross-court kills are almost always volleyed from above the waist, hitting downwards for a quick second bounce or nick. The *volley cross-court nick* is occasionally hit as a return of serve at the top levels of the game, and it is clearly a high-risk shot.

The opportunity to hit either of these shots is the reward of applying pressure on your opponent until you get the loose ball or he makes an unforced stroking error.

EIGHT RESPONSES TO VARIOUS SHOT SITUATIONS

In general, you are trying to hit the ball into a corner opposite where your opponent has just played his shot. Your next shot will also be influenced if your opponent hits a "loose" shot and gives you the chance to hit a forcing or finishing shot. Finally, you will want to watch your opponent as he anticipates your next shot and, if he commits by leaning too far, surprise him as described in several of these shot-response situations.

Response #1: Volley a Loose Cross-Court.

Opponent hits a loose cross-court or serve, you step across and volley the ball deep or volley drop.

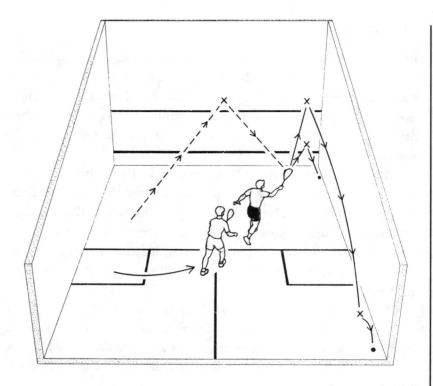

Response #2: Cross-Court a Poacher.

Opponent serves and moves past the middle, poaching into your shooting space because he expects another volley rail return. Chastise him with a deep cross-court.

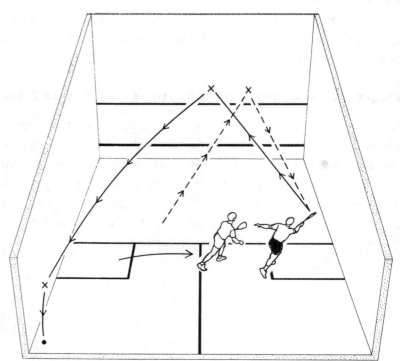

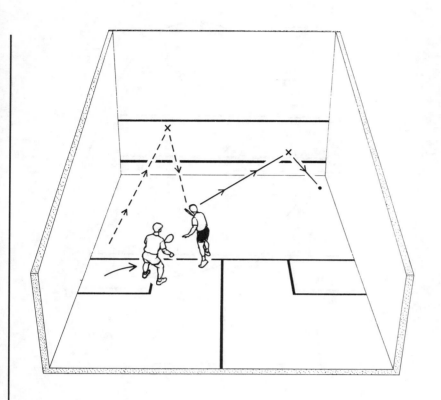

Response #3: Drop a Loose, Centered Ball. Opponent leaves a loose ball near the T. Move in front of him, keep him pinned behind and to the side and hit a cross-court drop shot.

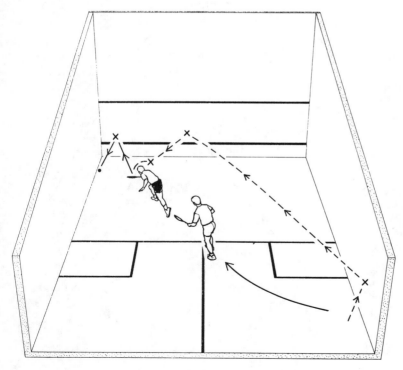

Response #4: Drop After a Back-Corner Boast. Opponent hits a defensive boast, you anticipate, move to front and hit a drop, forcing him to run the full diagonal of the court.

Response #5: Lob Over a Shadower.

Opponent hits a working boast and shadows you up to the front. Surprise him with a high cross-court to the opposite rear corner.

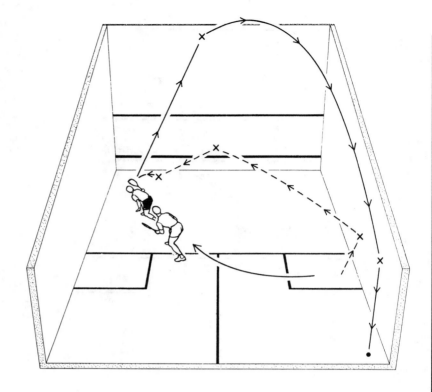

Response #6: Skid Boast Surprise.

Opponent hits a deep corner ball and moves to opposite front corner expecting a conventional back-corner defensive boast. Surprise him with a skid boast.

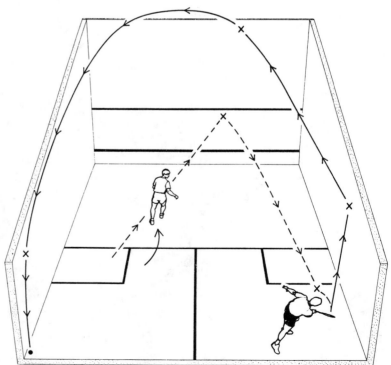

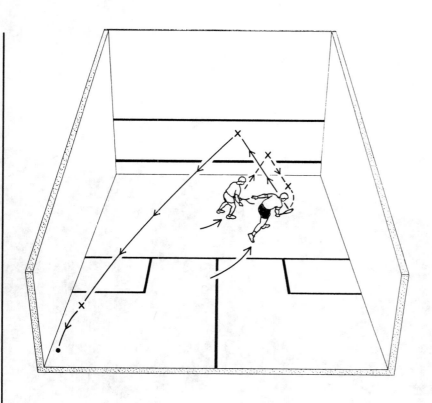

Response #7: Cross-Court a Loose Drop.
Opponent leaves a drop shot wide of the wall and stays short to cover his shot. Punish him with a deep cross-court.

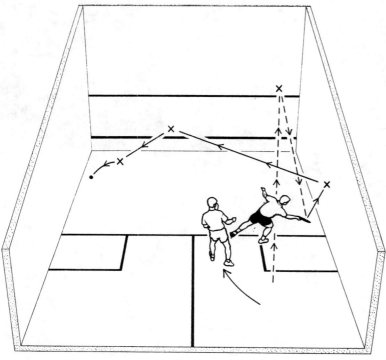

Response #8: Volley Boast a Loose Rail.
Opponent hits a loose rail. Step across and volley boast, sending him forward on the long diagonal.

Brett Martin (Australia) and Peter Marshall (England).

6. VOLLEYING AND SERVING

VOLLEY TO BE AHEAD

In soft ball, the volley keeps you ahead in the court and on the T. It keeps you ahead in putting pressure on your opponent. And it keeps you ahead, finally, in the point column.

If you are on the T, most loose shots that aren't very close to the wall or those that pass high overhead can be cut off and volleyed. A good volleyer can stay on the T for a long time, stretching his opponent to the limit. When you do so, you get to understand and relish what Jay Nelson means when he says, "I had him on a string!"

The volley can be hit defensively—when returning serve from the back court—or it can be hit offensively, say from mid-court as a *volley drop* or a *volley cross-court* into the nick.

"To be successful in soft ball—wide or narrow court—you must be aggressive," says Bob Callahan. "Look to volley, to cut the ball off early. Once you allow balls to take you to the back wall when you could have cut them off, you're going to lose. In hard ball, you can let shots go back because they more often pop up off the back wall and you can drive them comfortably off the back wall and not lose court position, not lose the offensive. In soft ball, you don't have that luxury. If you want to be a good player, you have to be going forward, forward, forward, and get the ball and cut it off. Don't allow yourself to be sucked to the back wall."

Demer Holleran encountered this concept on the court with the world's No. 4-ranked woman player, Sarah Fitzgerald. "She routinely beats me, she's really hard for me to play because she takes the ball very early and volleys extremely well, and there's no nonsense."

A British acquaintance of mine learned the same lesson from his school coach, who taught him after playing his shot to move forward and volley every time unless he couldn't reach the ball— even at the risk of hitting a weaker shot. A volley that gave his opponent less time was considered better tactics than taking the ball later and playing a stronger shot at the price of letting his opponent get back on the T.

To help you get into a volley mind set, think of soft ball as a *loopy* game. In hard ball, most of the balls you hit are moving fast and down below your waist. In soft ball, the cross-court, lob, skid boast, lob serve, and poorly hit rails send the ball looping through the middle tiers of the court. These balls can and must, as Callahan says, be cut off.

Paul Assaiante has further refined the concept of volleying in soft ball: "A big difference between hard ball and soft ball is that all the *finesse* shots you can play off a ground stroke in soft ball can also be played off a volley." A finesse shot is an angled shot requiring a high degree of racquet control. "In hard ball, the volley boast was a very risky shot, to be left for the Jon Fosters of the world and not for us mere mortals. But in soft ball, everyone, B and C players included, should already be using volley boasts because the ball is comparatively floating up there in the volley zone and because the volley boast is a whole lot easier to hit with the soft ball."

Paul gives this example of the need to adapt and volley: "Jim Zug has a great reverse corner that he takes just after the bounce

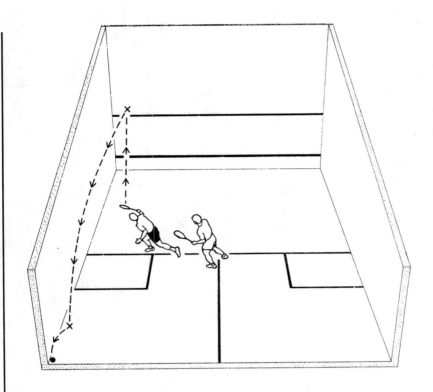

Volley Rail. The stance is more upright than for a rail or cross-court. Face the side wall, hit through higher with a more compact swing (shortening the stroke is almost automatic because you have less time). Hit with a punching kind of follow-through and a firmer wrist. Make contact with the ball opposite the leading shoulder and direct it to the target.

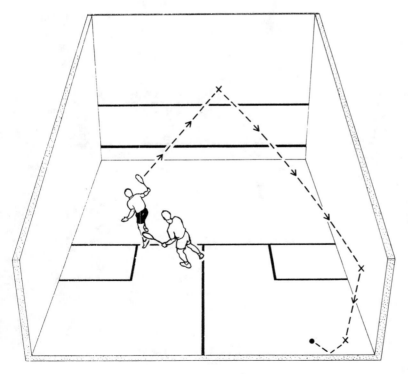

Volley Cross-Court. Intercept the ball a good bit earlier than for a volley rail and with a more open stance. The ball travels on a higher plane and can be hit with slightly less force than a cross-court drive. Targets at the rear are the same as for the drive.

**VOLLEYING
AND SERVING**

Straight Volley Drop.
This is a very effective finishing shot as it usually catches the opponent off-guard more than a ground-stroke drop shot would. The follow-through is less pronounced in order to kill the ball's pace—it's a sort of punching stroke which gives the shot its other name, the "stop volley."

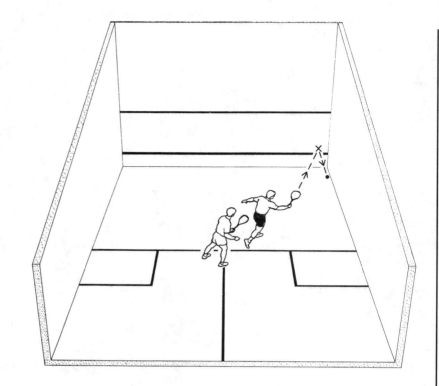

Volley Boast. This shot is a great one to use on a non-clinging serve or a short, high rail. Allow the ball to go a little past the point where you would hit a rail and direct the ball higher above the tin than you would on a working boast, i.e. hit it with plenty of margin for error. The ball should die before reaching the other side.

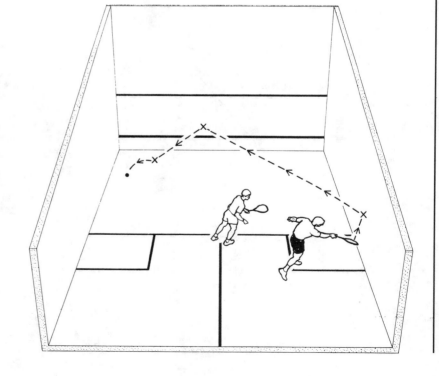

and buries. But all of a sudden, he's seeing every ball between waist- and shoulder-high, and his pet shot has been taken away. So he needs to learn to play that shot off the volley."

THE SERVE AS A MOMENT OF TRUTH

Squash is a delicate offensive/defensive ballet, mainly due to the fact that you share the same court space with your opponent. If one player is hitting slightly offensive shots, the other player is usually countering with slightly defensive shots. Or, at the extremes, one player is making "impossible gets" of the other's "sure winners."

Among advanced players, this principle of offensive/defensive balance is sustained over longer points. At lower levels of play, it is most critical at the beginning of each point—with the serve. It is estimated that a good soft-ball serve is worth three points a game at the top levels, and even more as you move down the ranks. And yet the serve is probably the most neglected part of the game. Perhaps this is so because practicing a squash serve is an awfully boring exercise.

Many players use the serve only to put the ball in play. This is a big mistake. It is your first opportunity to hit an offensive shot. If you can take the offense with the serve, then you are on top of the point from the very beginning. But if your serve is just a point starter, or worse, if you lay up a fat ball, someone with a good return of serve will get the first offensive shot. And that may set the tone for the entire point. Or it could end the point right there.

Most hard-ball players think you shouldn't hit a *lob serve* in soft ball because of the sloping, lower out-of-court lines, but they are misguided. The lob serve is actually a favorite among soft-ballers as the main attacking serve—for two reasons: one, a good lob is hard to return, as I explained in the previous chapter; and two, if you serve a forehand lob from the right-hand box, the extra 2 1/2 feet of international court width comes into full play, thus compensating for the lower lines by giving the ball a longer path to travel and drop before hitting the side wall. Jahangir Khan says of the lob serve from the right-hand box, "That's the

The Lob Serve. The serve is a hand-held volley with an open, cross-court stance. Toss the ball about a foot into the air, use a shortened stroke and follow through to the target. The ball should hit the front wall about three feet down and two feet left of center, barely skim the side high at the rear of the service box, then hit the floor before it reaches the back. Glide to the T and watch the opponent's return.

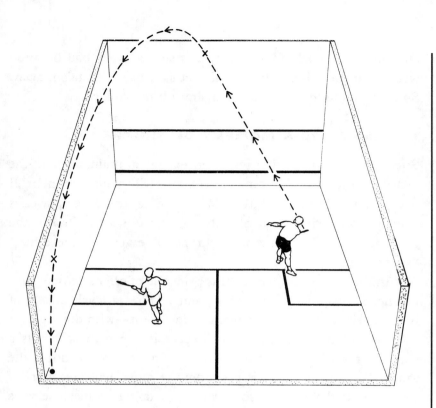

The Hard Serve. The stance here is more closed, as if you were hitting a forehand straight drive. Throw the ball up about a foot and hit a volley at shoulder height with a side wall target about three feet up (lower by half than the lob serve) and towards the rear of the service box. Vary the speed, angle, and height of the hard serve to keep the opponent off balance. Glide to the T and watch the opponent's return.

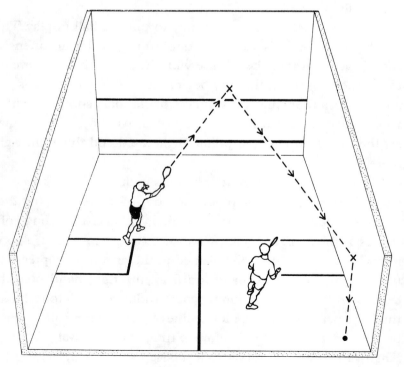

serve I favor from that side." Jonah Barrington, I was told by Jay Nelson, "would hit high soft serves to both sides and they were great."

The main alternative to the lob serve is the *hard flat serve,* usually preferred when serving forehand from the left-hand box. A lob serve from the left side is in greater danger of hitting the right side above the out-of-court line because the ball is being struck closer to the court's centerline, thus narrowing the angle to the right side wall and causing the ball to pass closer to that wall during more of its flight. It is for this same reason that you see a great many cross-court lobs and very few rail lobs in soft ball.

With both the lob and the hard serve, it is very important that you aim the ball to hit the side wall just *before* your opponent can volley it. Returning the ball after it angles off the wall is always harder than an in-line volley because your opponent has less time to line up his shot.

In the ballet of serve-and-return, the server wants to force a weak return and move into position to hit another forcing shot. To do this, the server must stroke and follow through in one fluid movement that ends on the T. This whole sequence can be rehearsed until it occurs naturally without thinking.

The receiver, on the other hand, wants to tip the balance back in his favor by intercepting the ball if at all possible before it strikes the side wall and volleying it deep back down the same wall and get on the T himself. There is a great symmetry here that you could think of as the Golden Rule of Squash—doing unto him what he so badly wants to do unto you.

The straight volley return of serve is *de rigueur* in squash, just as the King's Indian Defense is *the* response to the Queen's Pawn Opening in chess. The choice is clear: a volley rail return minimizes risk, maintains the balance, and keeps you out of trouble. It should be hit 80 to 90 percent of the time.

At other times, you would return the serve by hitting one of these options: a cross-court drive or a volley boast if your opponent is leaning with the expectation of another volley rail; a high cross-court lob if he is "cheating" forward; a volley straight drop;

or a volley cross-court nick, although this last option is a high-risk shot used by top players to finish the point. If you can't volley and the ball gets by you into the corner, your main choices of return are a straight rail, a cross-court drive, or the weakest return, a defensive boast.

A good rule to follow as receiver if the ball angles sharply off the side wall is to back with it—never turn—thus forcing your opponent out of the way behind you and giving you plenty of room to hit a rail or a drop.

Now, back to the serve. You should have a few variations to throw your opponent off when he has settled into a groove in returning your serve. These are some of the best alternative serves:

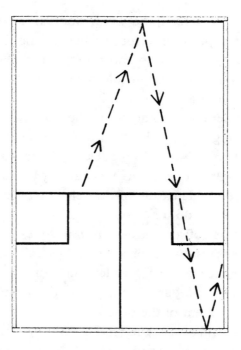

The Cling Lob. Hit this at a narrower angle than a regular lob serve to pass over the receiver's head, hit the back wall and continue angling towards the side wall before it bounces on the floor. The intent, as the name implies, is for the ball to cling to the side wall as it rebounds and cramp your opponent's return. Because it works best with a narrow angle, the cling lob should be used when striking the ball close to the centerline of the court, as in the forehand serve from the left-hand box.

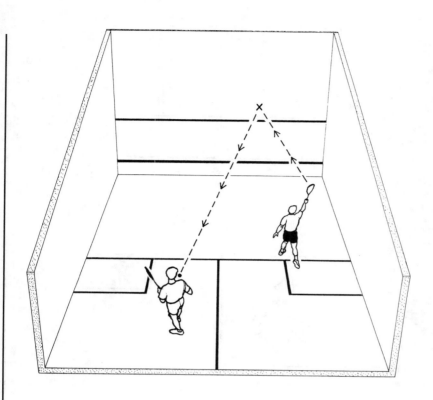

The Bodyline Drive.
Aim this hard serve directly at your opponent's shoulder, forcing him to adjust his position quickly or hit a very awkward return. In hard ball, some of the power servers could score points outright by hitting their opponent with the ball. In soft ball, this happens only if you catch your opponent daydreaming.

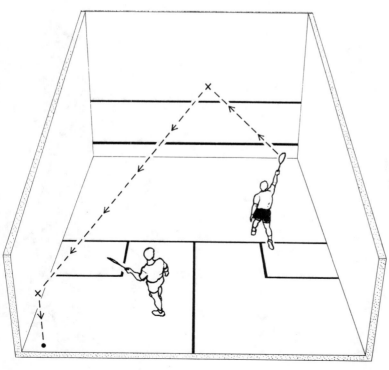

Smash-to-the-Nick.
Hit this serve the same as a tennis overhead smash, aiming to hit the side wall low and behind the service box, ideally to die in the side- or back-wall nick.

The Backhand. Use this serve from the right-hand box to narrow the angle off the front wall and shorten the move to the T. It also allows you to watch your opponent as you serve.

The Philadelphia. A lot of recently converted hard-ballers aren't even aware that you can hit this serve, which is also known as a reverse corner or Z-ball, in soft ball. Gary Waite, proficient with both balls, observes, "When you hit the Philadelphia serve in hard ball, you can hit it sidearm or overhead and the ball's speed will keep it on the same plane for quite a long time. When you hit it in soft ball, you need to hit up on it so that it's still traveling upwards after the side wall." The Philadelphia is usually hit forehand from the left-hand box, leaning far out towards the centerline and aiming high into the left-hand corner. The ball should hit high on the front wall very close to the side, rebound diagonally across court and hit the opposite wall, then angle parallel to the back wall. It is a difficult serve to hit and should be used only for its surprise effect.

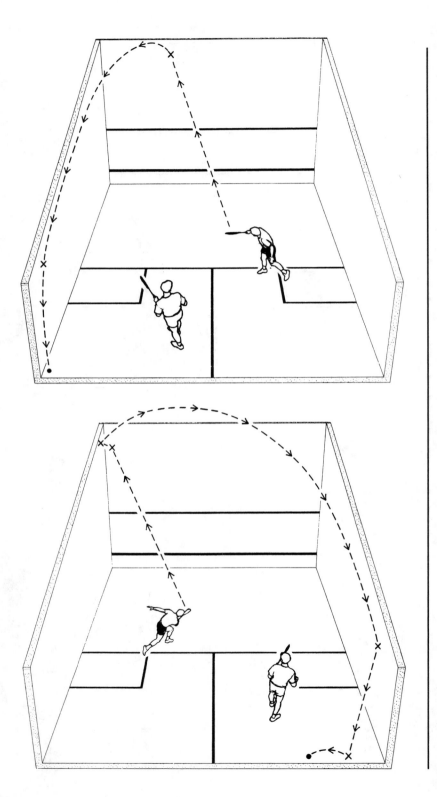

Rodney Eyles (Australia) and Chris Walker (England).

7. SHOT DRILLS

Nothing has changed since the time, twenty years ago, when Peter Briggs told me how he hit his shots. "Ask Sharif Khan what sort of shots he's going to hit, what his game plan is, and he'll tell you 'I just play.' And that's how I do it. I don't think beyond the shot I'm hitting. My game is purely reflexive. The ball's here, it's in a certain position, and I hit the shot. I really don't know why I hit it. I've played a lot, I know the game, and it just happens."

Of course, purely reflexive racquet work doesn't just happen. It is the product of long hours of drilling until you can hit the shots without thinking. Go back another twenty years before Briggs and what were they doing? "The best squash players," according to Cal MacCracken, "do a lot of practicing by themselves. Mateer, Salaun, and I used to do it. You take a ball, go in and go at it for an hour, and you come out absolutely dripping. You try all your shots. You set up certain routines, like hitting a reverse corner, so that you can hit them continuously without having to go chase the ball. You work out certain patterns just like a boxer who learns how to punch a punching bag. You learn certain exercises that approximate the speed and direction of the shot in the game, to help you get your timing and feel for the shot grooved into an automatic reflex."

And so it is today—even more so—because the soft-ball game is built on repetitive precision. "In soft ball, there's a tremendous premium if you can do the same thing from the same position, or with very little movement, again and again," says Frank Satterthwaite. "So when doing drills, the key is to make it a game of repetitive accuracy. If you can invent games to make it fun to hit with repetitive accuracy, it will be a lot easier for you to develop the skills that you need in actual match play to hit the same shot again and again without breaking down."

Once you have mastered a shot, to stay at or near your best performance level, you need to "rehearse" periodically. Being away from squash for even short periods can be frustrating because the motor coordination required for finesse and control is easy to lose. "That's why I feel I have to hit a squash ball almost every day," Goldie Edwards says. "I can't afford for my timing to go. For maximal events, like running, throwing, or jumping, where gross strength is so important, it doesn't matter as much."

Of the hundreds of solo, two-, and three-player practice drills, I have selected a dozen that will give any player a well-rounded arsenal of shots. Some drills involve modifications of the actual shot to create special repetitive routines so that practice can be continuous. Other drills can be devised simply by adding a feed ball to the shot diagrams shown in the previous two chapters.

All drills require that you have learned the technical aspects of hitting the shot from a pro, coach, or very good player. Someone must show you where to make contact with the ball, where the follow-through should be, whether to use spin, how hard you should hit, and so on. Once you know this, then you can begin practicing on your own.

A useful drilling technique is to use a slightly faster version of the ball than you would use in regular play. Jonah Barrington told Frank Satterthwaite that the top pros often practice with the faster red dot because it plays very similarly to the yellow dot in tournament conditions where the lights, people, and longer points keep the ball hot. Furthermore, the faster red dot helps improve your response times.

Another aid to drilling is the ball machine. If you can find a club or school that has one, it will consistently feed you balls and enable you to practice the often-encountered shot opportunities, such as the return of serve, much more efficiently.

While on the topic of the serve, it should be pointed out that the most neglected of all practice routines is the serve—a pity when you consider that a good serve can win points outright or at least put you on the offensive at the start of a rally.

Vic Niederhoffer used to practice or warm up right before a match by making random shots—into the corners, small cross-courts, rails, and volleys—that caused him to twist and turn his body continually during the routine. He did this mainly as a way of getting his eye on the ball. He also played make-believe matches against himself, as did Hashim Khan when he was mastering the game. Playing against yourself requires consummate skill and conditioning and qualifies as the ultimate form of practice.

SOLO DRILLS

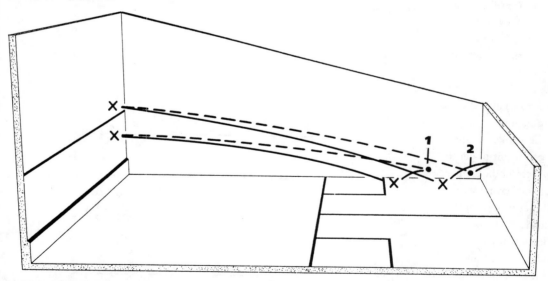

Drill #1: Rails. Stand at rear of service box, feed the ball off the side wall, and aim high enough on the front wall to first-bounce behind service box. Try to hit continuous rails until you can do 20-25 without breaking your rhythm. Keep the ball close to but off the side wall. Vary height, speed, and striking distance from the front wall to develop a sense of the correct depth for the first bounce in every situation. Try taking the ball (No. 1) before it hits the back wall, then (No. 2) after hitting it.

Drill #2: Cross-Courts.
Feed a rail and hit the
cross-court to angle off
the side wall low and
behind the service box.
Vary the height and
speed—a semi-lob
cross-court is a very
effective, energy-saving
shot.

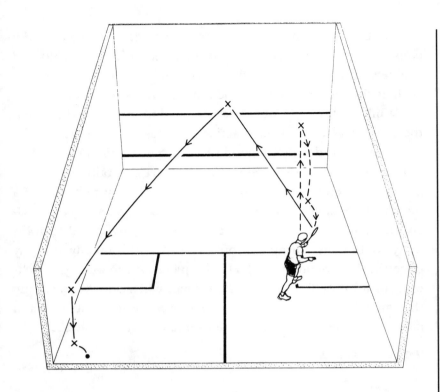

**Drill #3: Straight
Volleys.** Start close to
the front wall and hit
"pat" volleys (little
strokes). Your racquet
will be tilted back auto-
matically to get the cor-
rect arc. Keep stepping
back to change the
length, angle, and pace
of the stroke. Adjust the
target height to get the
correct depth. Concen-
trate on having your
racquet face meet the
outside of the ball (the
side closest to the side
wall) so it will hit the
front wall spinning
toward the side wall to
keep the ball hugging
the side wall. Hit con-
tinuously for consistent
accuracy; repeat on
both backhand and
forehand sides.

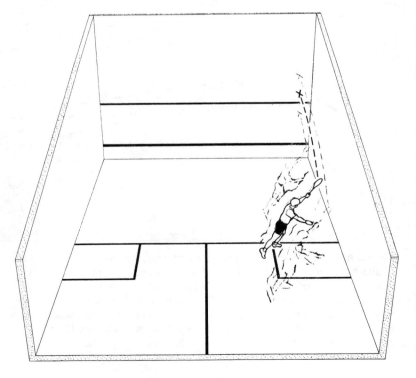

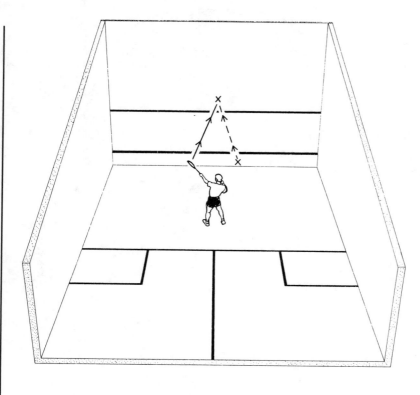

Drill #4: Cross-Court Volleys. Stand facing forward about two feet in front of the T and hit alternating forehand and backhand volleys, aiming always above the cut line. This drill can be done continuously without stopping to pick up the ball—it's a lot of fun, and quite hypnotic. The drill also works well with two players standing side by side, hitting alternate cross-courts.

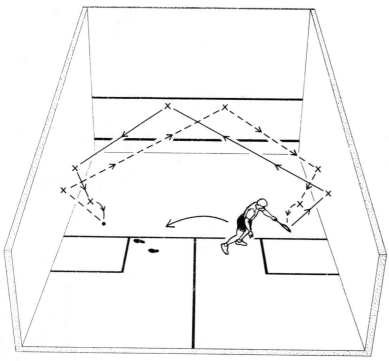

Drill #5: Boasts. This is a drill Jahangir Khan likes for solo boast practice. Feed the ball onto the forehand side near the service box, hit the boast with extra lift so that the ball reaches the backhand wall before bouncing twice. Run to that side, intercept, and hit a return boast to the forehand side. Keep it going.

SHOT DRILLS

93

Drill #6: Lob Stroke.
Paul Assaiante developed this drill to teach the very different lifting stroke for a high lob. Face the right-hand wall with your left foot forward. Feed a ball off the side and hit a forehand stroke gently upwards to a point high on the side, arching over, parallel to the end walls, to a point high on the other side. Turn and stand with the right foot forward, take the ball after it bounces once, and hit a backhand to reverse the ball's path to the beginning point. Turn and repeat. This is a continuous drill with emphasis on a soft upward stroke and an extra-high ball path.

Drill #7: The Butterfly. My fellow swimmer-turned-squasher Rick Carey named this drill. It grooves the difficult shot of hitting a cross-court into the nick. It can be hit as a ground stroke or, if you've got great hands, as a volley, never allowing the ball to bounce. The trick is to hit tight into the corners, front wall first, and pivot quickly to alternate forehand and backhand shots.

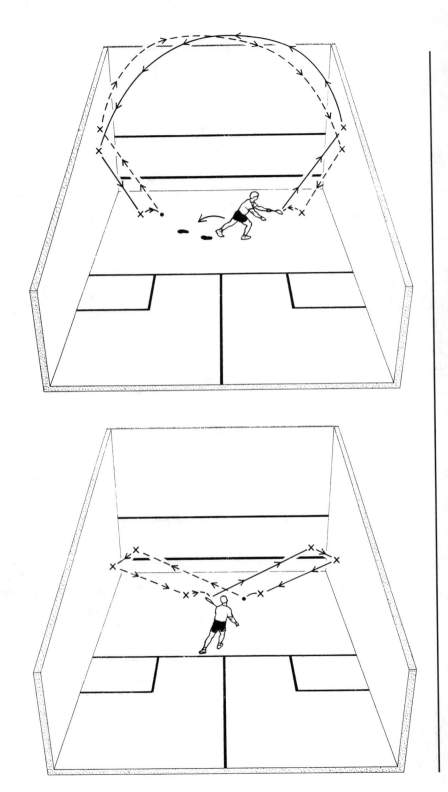

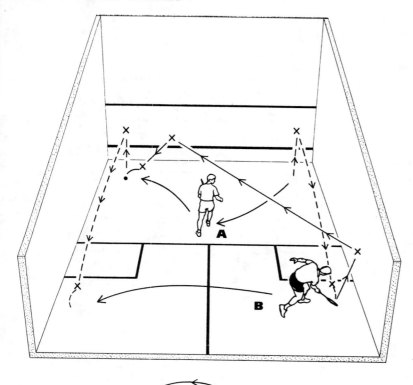

Drill #8: Rail/Boast.

This is a classic, continuous drill for two players, symmetrical and rhythmical. Player A hits a rail, B boasts, A moves over, takes the boast, and hits another rail, B moves over and boasts, and so on. Switch roles and repeat.

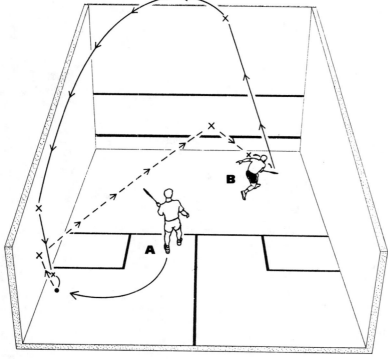

Drill #9: Boast/Lob.

Another continuous drill: player A feeds a ball off the wall and hits a boast, player B returns a high, cross-court lob, player A boasts, and so on. Switch roles and repeat.

SHOT DRILLS

Drill #10: Rail / Volley Cross-Court.

This is a more advanced drill that trains two players in the art of consistent stroking. Player A self-feeds and hits a high backhand rail, B moves across and volleys a backhand cross-court, A takes it on the bounce and hits a high forehand rail, B volleys a forehand cross-court, and so on. Switch roles and repeat.

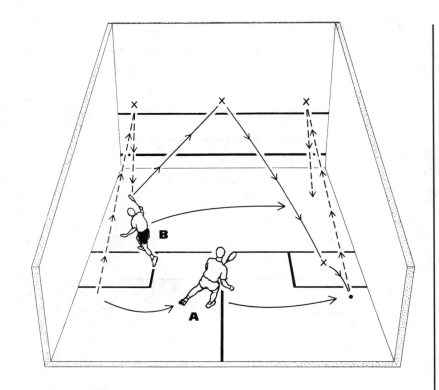

Mark Talbott (U.S.A.) and Rodney Martin (Australia).

8. SOFT BALL ON THE NARROW COURT

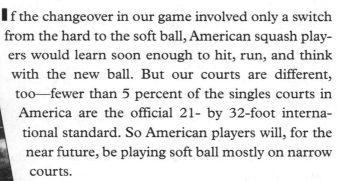

If the changeover in our game involved only a switch from the hard to the soft ball, American squash players would learn soon enough to hit, run, and think with the new ball. But our courts are different, too—fewer than 5 percent of the singles courts in America are the official 21- by 32-foot international standard. So American players will, for the near future, be playing soft ball mostly on narrow courts.

"Narrow" is a name of convenience that covers multiple differences in dimensions and court markings which, taken together, influence your choice of shots and game tactics. The major differences in the narrow court include: 2 1/2 feet less width, a higher out-of-court sideline, a higher service line and front wall, a T that is 4 feet closer to the back wall, and a 2-inch lower tin. (See court diagrams and specifications in Chapter 1.)

One of the hard-ball aficionados in defense of his game wrote in a letter to *Squash News* that "no one except for recreational players accepts narrow-court soft ball as a legitimate game." Richard Hankinson, assistant coach of women's squash at Princeton University, rose to the occasion with this rejoinder:

"This is nonsense. We have just completed the first year of inter-collegiate women's squash on narrow courts with the soft ball, and it proved to be one of the most exciting and competitive seasons ever."

Naturally, there are preferences for narrow or wide. Jay Nelson and Gary Waite play on both courts. "To say that soft ball is not a worthy game on the narrow court is silly," Jay says. "It may be too small for the Martin brothers or Jansher Khan, they're just such thoroughbreds athletically. I can imagine let after let after let." Gary leans the other way: "I've spent my life playing both hard ball and soft ball. I've played hard ball on the soft-ball court. I've played soft ball on the hard-ball court. However, I'll admit that it's not as enjoyable for me to play on the narrow court because it takes away a lot of width, which is a big element in the soft-ball game, cross-courts especially."

Virtually everyone agrees that there are differences in strategy on the two courts, so you need to be aware of these differences to play your best soft ball when you play on the narrow court. Here's what my experts advise:

Be more aggressive on the narrow court. *Paul Assaiante:* "I think you get payback for being shot-aggressive in the narrow court; because of the lower tin, because of higher lines on the side, you can lob more, you can boast more, and go short especially after a good lob, where on the wide court you need to be more conservative." *Frank Satterthwaite:* "You can be more aggressive in your shooting in a narrow court, you can put more emphasis on lobbing." *Mark Talbott:* "You can play fairly aggressively in the narrow court: you can attack the ball a lot more, volley more, go for a lot of short kills."

The very narrowness of it. *Jay Nelson:* "I find it very easy to play narrow-court soft ball. Maybe because it's narrow enough that the threat of the passing cross-court isn't there. I feel reasonably invulnerable in terms of being out-fitnessed. The guy's going to have to beat me with drop shots. Now, the drop shot is a much more powerful tool on the narrow court because there's a lower tin, and because of a subtlety that a lot of players don't pick up—the striker can cover the responses to his drop shot more readily.

You can cover the re-drop and at the same time cover almost any cross-court. The retriever doesn't have to worry too much about getting passed with a cross-court because the narrowness of the court prevents that."

Hitting cross-courts on the narrow court. *Bob Callahan:* "I think you can still use cross-courts on the narrow court, but it's got to break deep enough to take your opponent into the back corner. It's easier for him to cut it off because it passes the short line heading for the side wall much closer to a player standing on the T. So you have to hit it crisply. A good cross-court on a wide court puts your opponent much more on the defensive than a good cross-court on the narrow."

Differences related to the T. *Mark Talbott:* "On the narrow court, I would stand about a foot in front of the T; on the wide court, I would stand a foot or two behind it. Be careful not to hit too many cross-courts because it's easy to volley in the narrow court. I can stand in that narrow court and cut off any soft-ball cross-court if I put my mind to it, so you have to hit it nice and high." *Frank Satterthwaite:* "It's easier to control the T on a narrow court. If I'm in front of you, it's much harder for you to get out from behind me. Conversely, it's very hard to drive your opponent off the T, so hit a lot more lobs, particularly down the wall—use lobs to get back on the T."

"It's a front-and-back game." *Jay Nelson:* "The cross-court return of serve is out. It's a mistake I make all the time. That's my natural inclination. I have to go on court and say '95 percent, 95 percent, 95 percent down-the-line volley.' I have to keep reminding myself of that return of serve. A lot of times I'm just hitting what I call three-quarter speed, nothing balls, aimed above the service line, just trying to hit a glue, that's all, challenge the guy." *Emily Goodfellow:* "We try to encourage our players to cheat forward. Chances are you aren't going to be beaten by some great length shot to the back. Power isn't as much a factor; therefore, protect the front of the court, get your weight forward, because you will get burned on the straight drop or the trickle boast if you're camped out in the back. Get your heels on the T, not your toes, and cut that ball off." *Ned Edwards:* "Soft ball on a narrow court is a much more front-and-back [parallel to the side walls] game. The idea of width and being able to play the ball to width does not serve you well. If your man is anywhere near the center, it's going to be awful tough for the soft ball to pass him. The court's just not wide enough to spread him out."

Hit the higher shots. *Neil Pomphrey:* "You can bail out from a dangerous situation in the front court by lobbing it down the same side wall, because of the extra height of the out-of-court lines." *Craig Thorpe-Clark:* "There needs to be more emphasis on lobs. Lob and drop more to use the length of the court." *Emily Goodfellow:* "We also teach our players to use the higher side lines and hit a straight lob. From up front, you can hit a really good high lob straight down the line and it'll go right high and not go out; it'll drop right into the corner. That's a lethal shot on the narrow court. Furthermore, the serve is an enormous offensive weapon on the narrow court. You have to use the height of the narrow court. And if the court also has a high ceiling, you can really put an aggressive lob serve into the back without risking a point. We spend a lot of time working on lob serves for that reason." *Jay Nelson:* "If you make that high serve good enough, you can cause a lot of trouble. It's riskier, but if you can drop it in, you create severe problems for the guy. There is much more latitude to hit the lob serve in the narrow court because of the higher lines. It may just drop in and become almost unhittable. Coming from hard ball on a narrow court, you don't think about lobs. Look at soft-ball players on the wide court—they lob a lot. In fact, I think you should lob even more with soft ball on the narrow court."

Boasts, angles, and the three-wall nick. *Richard Hankinson:* "I find that you can hit very good aggressive boasts from the back, like flat boasts, and they nick in the opposite corner. And they're great shots. If you do that same shot on a wide court, you're dead. It never makes the other side wall. On the wide court, I teach our players to open the racquet and boast high so the ball floats and comes out. Don't hit aggressively. On the narrow court, go for it. You can hit some winners. *Paul Assaiante:* "In the narrow court, the boast is still a three-wall shot—you need that third wall to get the ball to die faster. You can hit a three-wall from deep and it will carry across the narrower width, ending up like a three-wall shot with the hard ball, whereas you can't hit that shot in the wide court." *Jay Nelson:* "The three-wall nick works on the narrow court. I've come from the wide court and played a guy who is a very hard hitter and he beat me with three-wall nicks. Also, the working boast because of the lower tin: you can hit it low and hard and it really works. You can hit it from deep, say, if you're having a fairly long point, kinda cat-and-mouse, he hits a rail that's not too good, you show a rail—just kaboom!—into the side and low. If you get him to step wrong, it's going to be a winner. One more thing, the reverse corner can be used selectively on the narrow court, and you can get an advantage with it. On the wide court, if you hit it, you're history, because the wider angle makes the ball come more out into the center and the higher tin produces a real fat ball."

Volleying and your skill level. *Demer Holleran:* "If you're an average player, you should volley as much as you can, get in front of your opponent and use your short shots when you get the chance because the short shots are so much more effective on the narrow court. If you are a better player, meaning you can run almost everything down, I recommend playing a slower game, play more lobs, look for the chance to hit a volley drop, because in the narrow court you can cut the ball off so much easier and if you hit a volley drop with your opponent behind you, the ball's two inches closer to the floor. On the narrow court, the straight volley drop is a real winner."

In summary, the narrow court creates limitations and opportunities. You should avoid cross-court drives and returns of serve. You should emphasize playing forward, volleying, going short when in front, lobbing more on serve and during the rally, using the lob/drop combination, hitting the occasional three-wall nick and reverse corner, and generally playing more aggressively to end points sooner than you would on the wide court.

Narrow-Court Straight Lob. Take advantage of the higher side lines and hit the straight lob as an offensive shot.

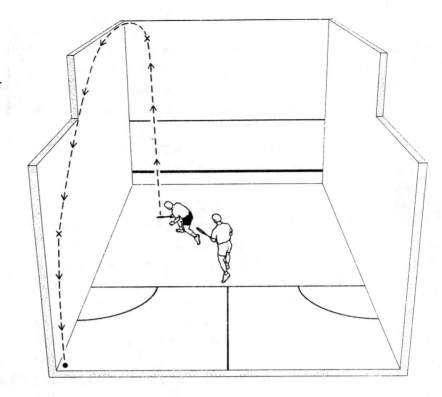

Narrow-Court Three-Wall Boast. The three-wall boast can also be hit as an offensive shot due to the greater probability that it will carry across and catch the third wall, possibly even hitting the nick.

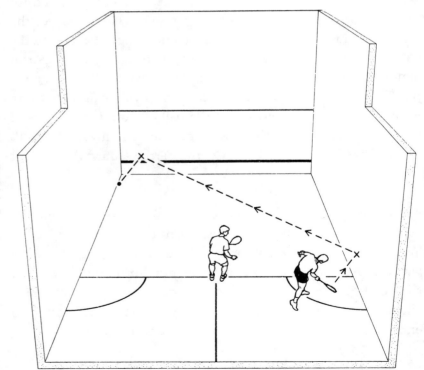

Narrow-Court Reverse Corner.
This is a favorite shot of hard-ballers and can still be hit on the narrow court, being careful to do so only when your opponent is behind you.

Brett Martin (Australia), foreground, and Rodney Eyles (Australia).

9. OFF-COURT PREPARATION

CONDITIONING FOR ENDURANCE

In squash there is as much running as in soccer or basketball, but you cannot be substituted for. And it's much faster than tennis, with a lot less time between points. So if you want to play your best squash, you must be in good physical condition.

One of the reasons the Pakistanis have dominated squash is that they learn the game at high altitudes. Playing in thin air, they develop tremendous lung capacity. When Hashim Khan came on the scene, we suddenly became aware of a new standard of conditioning. With his huge lungs and barrel chest, he could run all day on a squash court and never take a fast breath.

Today's soft-ball champions are even more fit than Hashim. They reveal the link between endurance and motivation. Brett Martin more or less threw down the gauntlet to American players when he told me, "The main thing hard-ball players don't have is confidence in keeping the ball going. They want to end the rally, whereas in soft ball you have to believe that you can keep going, believe in your fitness. You have to train your mind to say, 'I'm not going to die, I can keep going.'

"When I first came on the tour, I went out there and I tried to play hard but I didn't know what hard was. I'd get blown out after maybe winning the first game and doing well in the second and, all of a sudden, my lungs started burning and I thought I was going to die, but I didn't. The next time I was able to go a little longer, until gradually I built my pyramid bit by bit and could stay on with any of the other players. I think that's the main difference between what I've seen with the hard-ball and the soft-ball players."

There are two principal types of cardiorespiratory exercises that will help build the endurance to carry you through long rallies: aerobic and anaerobic. You need some of both for the best results.

Aerobic exercises use energy derived from oxygen sources, so you must be able to take in enough oxygen during the exercise to keep restoring the energy base. A two-mile run is an ideal aerobic exercise. Jumping rope at a pace similar to the running would also qualify, if you preferred that or could not get outdoors. Running distance, jumping time, and frequency should vary with age and the desired level of conditioning. Two to three times a week will maintain a good "club match" level of endurance.

Anaerobic exercises use energy that does not depend on the recovery of oxygen. If you run flat out up and down the squash court, as you must in some points, you will have used up all of your oxygen reserves, without restoring them, in as little as 35 to 40 seconds. Your legs ache, you are gasping for air, and you can't go on until you have replenished your oxygen. During an intense squash rally, players' heart rates will reach 80 percent to 85 percent of maximum and they will be in the anaerobic range, contrasted with 60 percent to 80 percent during aerobic exercise.

David Behm, in his application of advanced training techniques to squash, points out that very fit squash players who train at increasingly higher intensities can actually play aerobically when their heart rate is above 80 percent of maximum—in effect moving their anaerobic threshold upwards. One of the techniques he uses to achieve this training effect is to simulate the alternating rhythm of intense rallies followed by brief periods of rest on the stairmasters, bicycles, and other machines his players use for fitness training. To follow this routine, you would start at a level compatible with your current fitness and build up gradually from shorter periods of flat-out intensity alternating with longer periods of rest, to longer intense periods and shorter rest periods. You repeat this on-off rhythm for 10–15 minutes. For example, you might go flat out for 15 seconds then go easy for 30–45 seconds, gradually building up to 30–45 seconds of flat-out intensity alternating with easy periods of 15–30 seconds.

Two other well-tested ways of building anaerobic fitness are court sprints and 440-yard sprints. In the court sprints, you run the length of the squash court as many times as you can in one minute, touching the wall tin-high at each end. Rest for 45 to 60 seconds and repeat, building up to 15–20 sets. World-class players such as Chris Dittmar run at least 20 lengths of the court in a minute. Some of the fastest and fittest have been known to run up to 28 lengths in a minute.

Geoff Hunt became famous for running repetitive 440-yard sprints to build his anaerobic base. At the top level, he and other players might run a 440 in 60–70 seconds and walk for 90 seconds, repeating the sprint/walk interval 10 to 15 times.

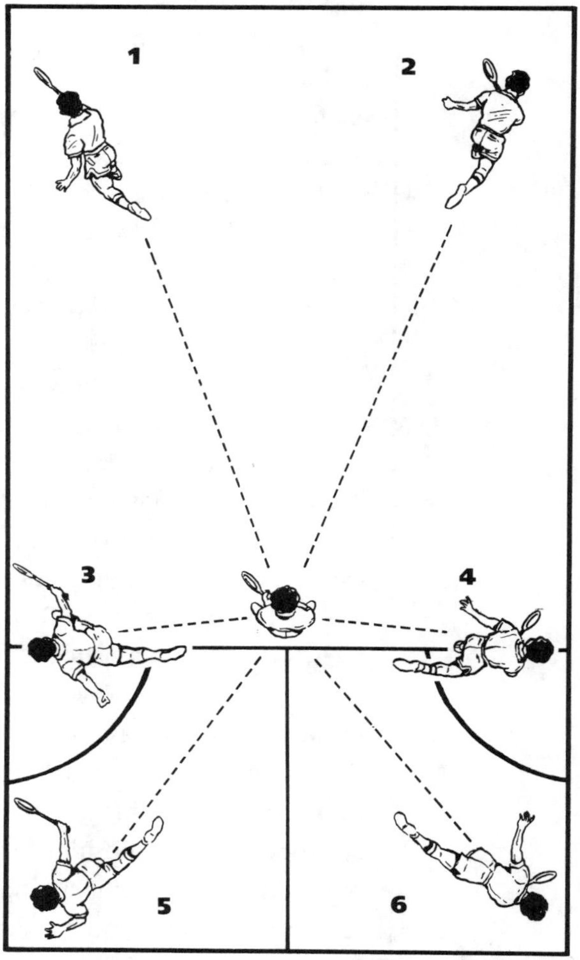

Fig. 7. Six-Point Drill.

The six-point drill (Figure 7) is a special type of anaerobic conditioner for squash players. It takes ten to fifteen minutes and can be worked in after an easy match or following a practice session. You go on the court by yourself and start at the T with your racquet in the ready position as if you were waiting there for an opponent to return your deep rail shot.

Begin by moving in long, quick strides to the front left corner, stretch and hit an imaginary rail shot, rebound and backpedal in long steps to the T. Repeat to the front right corner and return to the T. Move laterally and hit a "volley," return to the T, and repeat on the opposite side. Go back into each corner and hit a "rail" or a "boast." Return to the T and start over. Cover each numbered point three times for one set. This is a simulated point. Rest for 30 seconds and repeat. A male college player in peak trim can do ten sets, 40 seconds each, with 30-second rest intervals. A forty-year-old businessman in good playing shape should be able to do six to eight sets, 50 seconds each, with 40-second rest intervals. Women's times would be about 5 to 10 seconds slower in each case.

Norm Peck, former men's coach at Princeton University, said of his players, "What this means, if they can do ten hard sets, is that they can play ten very hard points consecutively. And most players cannot play ten straight hard points. In fact, I've yet to see a player who does not train in this manner who could play even three very hard points in a row. By hard points I mean points that are going to take you all over the court, that are going to last twenty-five to thirty shots."

For a mid-level player, the six-point drill is also an excellent way to develop "court presence," by being careful in terms of foot position, staying down on the shot, and executing a good stroke. It makes you determine and practice which foot to start with to arrive at proper stroking positions in the extremes of the court. If you are often late on your backswing, you should strive to feel the counterthrust of your racquet moving backward as your body moves forward. You should also try to reach each of the six points with as few steps as possible. Try to execute this drill in long, flowing strides.

A PROGRAM FOR SQUASH MUSCLES

"In squash, the single most important ingredient after skill is strength," says Goldie Edwards. "That's what's wrong with half of our women players. They can't even do push-ups—just lifting part of their own body weight.

"Look at the Aussie squash players, their women in particular, and see how strong they are compared to our squash players. The same was true of tennis thirty years ago. They were beating us with regularity. Then Billie Jean King and Stan Smith found out how they were training, both for endurance and strength, and we turned it around.

"Getting a little stronger, getting that one extra thing going for you in addition to your skill, putting that together with squash, improves the squash. The deep shots are stronger, the hard serve is stronger, the endurance is greater, you are quicker and faster.

"When you don't use your muscles, they start losing strength after about forty-eight hours. This happens at all ages, though it is more pronounced as you grow older. If you engage in a bout of exercise, or a bout of squash, or a bout of anything, you will get microscopic biochemical and physiological changes within your muscles. These changes will reverse themselves after about two days of inactivity. That's why most physical conditioning programs are done three days a week. That's why a football player at Pitt starts doing exercises the very next day after a knee operation. A guy in the street who doesn't know this or who doesn't have a doctor who knows about exercise, he's still limping around a year later.

"If you consider yourself an athlete, your musculoskeletal apparatus is your tool, and you have to pay attention to it and cultivate it in order for it to deliver its full potential."

When Goldie is not on a squash court, she teaches future teachers of physical education and conducts other college and graduate courses in tension control, health maintenance, and health improvement. On one of her sabbatical leaves she studied under Dr. Hans Kraus, specialist in physical medicine, world-renowned expert on muscle ailments and rehabilitation, and former member of the President's Council on Physical Fitness and Sports. When I was researching this aspect of the game, I went to Dr. Kraus and asked him to help me develop an exercise program for squash muscles.

Dr. Kraus started by giving me a brief refresher course on the way muscles produce body movements. One muscle or muscle group contracts while an opposing muscle relaxes. For example, to bend your arm at the elbow, your biceps contract while your triceps relax, and to straighten it again, the biceps relax while the triceps contract. If both sides of the muscle "team" are not cooperating, then the desired motion is impaired.

Thus, a backswing, forehand, and follow-through depend just as much on the muscle's ability to give up contraction at the right time and in the right amount as they do on muscle strength. This aspect of flexibility enables the muscle to be strong through its full range of motion.

Loose, flexible muscles are so important to athletic performance and the avoidance of injury that you should begin any workout, practice, or match with relaxing and stretching exercises before even starting to warm up. For the best muscle condition you should also stretch and relax after cooling off from playing or exercising. I have constructed a mnemonic device for this routine called "Muscle Hill," shown in Figure 8.

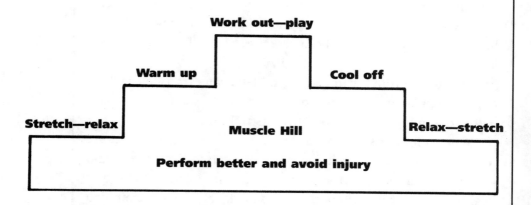

Fig. 8. Muscle Hill.

First, let's take the *stretching* exercises (Figure 9).

Dr. Kraus recommended thirteen of these in the sequence shown. Each will stretch the muscles associated with one or more body joints. To get the best value from these exercises, it is important to stretch beyond the point of easy performance, to feel the pull in your muscles well past the range in which you normally use them. In fact, you should stretch until you are stopped by the mechanical limitations of your joints or the elasticity of your muscles. This does not mean that you should stretch violently or to the point of pain. Continual stretching over time will increase your range of movement in each joint and improve the flexibility of all these muscle groups. You will reap substantial benefits in your stroke production, reduced exposure to injury, and general well-being off the court.

Flexibility is far more important in the soft-ball game than it was in hard ball, with the lunging and stretched-out stroking, retrieving shots in the front of the court, recoiling to the T—all over much longer points. To reach the top in world soft ball, players start early in their careers, visiting physiologists and designing individualized stretching programs to develop and prepare their bodies properly.

"You watch a guy like Jansher Khan move around the court," says Gary Waite. "That is years and years of flexibility work, patterns of movement, balance, strength work in the right places. He looks like a wimpy guy, but he's strong."

Before getting into the frequency and duration of the stretching exercises, let's look at their companion group of *strengthening* exercises (Figure 10).

The first fourteen of these fifteen use dumbbells, the last one, the weight of your own body. Once again, these exercises should be done in the sequence shown.

When lifting weights for strength, there is a generally held misconception, according to Dr. Kraus, that it is better to lift lighter weights more times than it is to lift heavier weights fewer times. Many people think that heavy weights produce tight muscles. This is not true. Tight muscles, as far as weight lifting is concerned, come from lifting too rapidly or from repeating the same exercise too many times without changing. Generally speaking, many repetitions with low weight increase endurance rather than strength. Only by lifting increasingly heavier weights will your muscles continue to get stronger.

Fig. 9. Stretching for Squash.

(relax after each exercise, breathe deeply throughout)

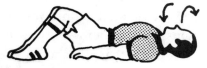

1 Breathe, relax, turn neck to both sides

2 Knee lift . . .

. . . and drop

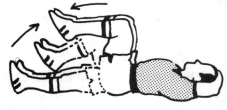

3 Heel slide

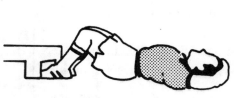

4 Sit-ups . . .

. . . with knees flexed

5 Kneeling pectoral stretch

6 Trapezius stretch

7 Standing pectoral stretch

8 Soleus stretch

9 Calf muscle and Achilles stretch

10 Floor touch

11 Hamstring stretch

12 Groin muscle stretch

13 Crossed hands, floor touch, and swivel—stretches everything

**Fig. 10.
Upper-Body
Strengthening
for Squash.**

1 Curls

2 Reverse curls

3 Front elevations

4 Side elevations

5 Hands behind neck and back

**6 Wrist curls
and rolls**

7 Bent-over one-arm rowing

8 Bent-over extensor lift

9 Hands across chest and out to side

SMART
SQUASH

116

10 Bent-over side lifts

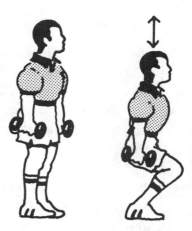

11 Half knee-bends

12 Alternative overhead press

13 Full press

14 Bench press

15 Push ups

Brett Martin uses a lot of heavy weights in his strength training. He says, "I think it is very important to keep your whole body strong, which a lot of squash players have trouble with. Their bodies fall apart because some parts are strong and some are not. Some players, the right side of their body is overdeveloped and the left is underdeveloped. That's just asking for back trouble. You've got to get your whole body symmetrically strong."

The recommended approach to a weight-lifting workout is to begin by relaxing and stretching as before, and then, with a relatively light weight, do three or four of each exercise, and go through the entire set of exercises; then start all over again with a heavier weight. Build up to your level of tolerance, then taper off with lighter and lighter weights until you are back where you started. Stretch your muscles, relax, and your weight-lifting workout is complete. You will have climbed Muscle Hill.

It is important when doing the stretching and strengthening exercises to let go and relax, momentarily, after each one. The muscles need to "go loose" after each movement. By doing this, instead of keeping the muscles continually in a tensed state, you maintain the desired suppleness.

The best players today are the professionals or quasi-pros who are able to undergo more intensive training than yesterday's part-time athletes. They have learned how to listen to their bodies. This improves their chances of avoiding injury as they strive to increase their stamina for the marathon points and games now typical in soft ball.

Injuries will happen, regardless, and when they do, you need the right regimen and attitude to come back. The story of Goldie Edwards, who recently came back from a knee injury at age sixty, to continue playing at the top levels in U.S. women's squash, is exemplary. Goldie worked back gradually, at first running in the water with a wet vest, then running up hills and walking back down, until she could get back on the court and begin hitting the ball and doing court routines.

One of her doctors advised her to hang up her racquet, that she had had a good, long career and should retire. "I was so angry. When I was able to play again, I wanted to go back to him and show him, but I wouldn't bother. As I said before, it's my mental health. Women and men see me play and they say to me 'I can't believe you're as old as you are.' And some of them have gone out to take lessons as a result of me playing. I think that's terrific, if I can go on being a model, because I still have such fun!"

WHAT TO EAT BEFORE A MATCH

If you have a big match coming up, how soon do you start paying attention to how much and what type of food is in your body? When, in effect, do you go on a "match diet?"

Vic Niederhoffer liked to have meat eight or nine hours ahead and a lot of carbohydrates such as mashed potatoes, spaghetti, or bread a few hours before he played. Between two matches on the same day he stuck mainly with juices and carbohydrates. Today's champions have not improved on this basic pre-match regimen.

Bob Callahan agrees that carbohydrates should be the main ingredient of your last meal before a match. He advises his Princeton players to stay away from fatty foods. "We make sure to have lots of bagels around, fruits, and juice, especially for between matches, when there is not much time to eat. We ask all the players to eat three hours before they play."

David Behm mixes half orange juice with half water and drinks one glass 30 minutes before a match, another before each of the second and third games. The fructose in fruits, and their juices is a source of carbohydrates. David observed that recently exercised muscles accept carbohydrates more readily and that you should eat fruit or drink orange juice within 45 minutes of the end of a match. In especially hot conditions, he advises cold drinks to bring the body's core temperature down more quickly.

You should know the following facts as a background for understanding your needs for certain foods. First, the physical demands of squash deplete your body's stores of sugar, salt, water, and other substances. These need to be replaced in varying amounts and intervals, depending on the degree of depletion and your playing schedule.

Carbohydrates turn into glucose (body sugar) when digested. Glucose is converted into glycogen, which is stored in your liver and muscles. Glycogen is the body's basic muscle fuel. There is normally enough glycogen in your cells to fuel about three hours of squash, so the average player doesn't have to worry. But for two matches in one day, or for top-level marathon rallies, a player must replace the glycogen stores. Fructose, or fruit sugar, as found especially in honey and to a lesser extent in fruit juices, promotes a rapid replacement of depleted glycogen reserves.

There is a training technique known as *glycogen boosting* that can be useful to players who regularly get into long, hard matches. Taking advantage of this technique involves three steps: first, you exhaust your glycogen reserves with a particularly long match or other type of workout, usually accompanied by a lot of sweating. Then you eat only proteins and fats for two or three days. Finally, you eat mainly carbohydrates for two or three days. At this point your glycogen level should be nearly double its normal level, and you are ready for the "big match." Remember, though, that glycogen boosting isn't really needed at less than the highest tournament levels.

Replacing salt is most effectively confined to using it on your food. However, if you are playing in hot courts, or otherwise lose an unusual amount of water during a match, you may also wish to use one of the electrolyte drinks during or right after a hard match to replace lost sugar, salt, magnesium, potassium, and water. Salt tablets are no longer accepted as the best way to replace lost salt. Vitamin C has come back into favor as a strengthener of the immune response to upper respiratory infections. And women players should add some form of iron supplement on a regular basis.

For women squash players, Goldie Edwards believes that there is no need to overload on carbohydrates. "Very few women's matches last longer than an hour," she says. "Now I feel good if I've had some carbohydrates, but if I've had too much, my mouth gets dry. And I feel thirsty. That's because carbohydrates actually absorb fluid from the tissues."

At a tournament, you often have to eat what's available, what they are serving. Goldie tries to stay away from fat. "I try to keep away too from things like lettuce and cabbage, things that might be gas-forming in the intestines. I'll go for rolls. Very often at these tournament luncheons they serve chicken in some form, and that I usually find fine. If there's a nice ripe banana around, I eat that. I drink tea or coffee. Strangely, if the coffee is decaffeinated, I get a headache.

"Chocolate bars, you know, are high in fat. And they make you very thirsty. The other thing is, people who drink Cokes and eat a lot of candy bars before they play can induce what is tantamount to insulin shock in themselves. It works this way: You drink maybe a couple of Cokes and then you go on and play, and about twenty minutes into the game, you get a weakness, and you feel a bit jittery. What happens, you see, is that you bump up the blood sugar level very high with this sucrose, with this sugar in the Coke, and you feel really good for a little while, and then the pancreas comes along with an outpouring of insulin, and the insulin takes out the blood sugar, which it is supposed to do, but you have overstimulated the pancreas. So you produce a lot of insulin, and it really lowers the blood glucose level to below what it was, and if you're not careful it can put you in the hypoglycemic range, and that's when you feel the dizziness and weakness. That will pass when you mobilize your own stores to right it again. It's something that various people are sensitive to, and they can never understand why this has happened."

MENTAL PRACTICE

"When I was learning squash, I did a lot of mental practicing," Goldie Edwards recalled. "I found the balls off the walls very difficult, and I didn't know which way to move. The ball would be going one way, I'd move toward it, and it would come off into me. So I began visualizing, between on-court sessions, what I was doing wrong, and I would picture myself making the correct move in the same situation. I can't tell you how much that helped. Now, years later, I still use this technique to improve my stroking and shotmaking."

Mental practice is an old concept that has gained popularity under such new names as "body thinking," and "visuomotor behavior rehearsal." Basically it consists of relaxing, screening out other stimuli, and rehearsing an activity in the mind. One of the memorable incidents of its success occurred when Jean-Claude Killy, the legendary French skier, while recovering from an injury, prepared for one of his races by skiing it mentally, and nothing more. The race turned out to be one of his best. Since then, mental practice has been used successfully by American Olympic skiers and marksmen to prepare psychologically for their events.

The reason mental practice works can be demonstrated scientifically. In the context of squash, say that you decide to hit a backhand. A series of electrical impulses flows from your brain via motor nerves to the correct muscles, telling some to shorten and others to lengthen, which results in the basic movements for a backhand stroke. At the same time these impulses are on their way to the muscles, another part of the brain—call it the "shot memory"—compares its version of the backhand to where your arm, racquet, and the ball are, and sends signals to make last-minute adjustments to your stroke. The more you have practiced, the better picture you have of the stroke in your shot memory, and the better these last-minute adjustments are.

Take the problem many squash players have when receiving the serve. They wait with wrist cocked and the racquet in ideal position, but the grip is iron tight and *all* arm muscles are in advanced degrees of tension. In other words, the arm is rigid, as if momentarily set in concrete. Before the serve can be returned, they must cancel the signals stiffening the arm and send out new ones for the appropriate service-return motions.

If these same players were to return serves in mental practice, with the goal of obtaining a firm grip and relaxed arm as they are waiting for the ball, and if electrodes were attached to measure the motor nerve impulses, they would in most cases experience a shift away from the electromyograph pattern for a tight arm to those for a loose arm. Repetitions of these mental rehearsals have been shown to strengthen and reinforce these nerve impulse patterns and in effect preprogram the nerve channels for the desired muscle action.

Thus, electromyographically, if you visualize a forehand, the bursts of nerve impulses are the same in microscopic form as if you were actually hitting the forehand.

So, once you know the stroke basics, you can begin practicing them mentally. As Goldie explains it, "First I try to be very relaxed, usually by sitting with my eyes closed. If you really understand the stroke, you can form a clear mental picture of it. Then I think my way through each phase of the stroke. I can see myself doing it, and I check the various reference points. I check the grip, the stance, shoulder position, where the racquet is on the backswing, position of the wrist and forearm, the ideal contact position, and the follow-through. I can actually visualize myself meeting the ball. The more times I do that, the less I have to think about it on the court.

"In mental practice I think myself through a situation on the court. I go through the options. I visualize where the other person would be and choose the shot. Then I execute the shot, noticing the path of the ball in relation to the court.

"Some people never think about these things between games. They wait and try to get it all together when they go on the court. I think you have to be *ahead* of the game, so that when the situation arises, you are programmed and ready to go."

SEX BEFORE SQUASH?

The question arises more frequently now, both with the growth of participant sports and with the entry of women into formerly male-dominated sports: Does sex before play improve your game? There are some strongly held views on the subject, and there have been several magazine articles by physicians that reflect a net positive view toward the effects of sex on athletic performance.

Reliable research is hard to come by on this subject. Had Masters and Johnson or Dr. Ruth been squash players, we might not still be in the dark over the solution to this intriguing problem.

However, until such time as a definitive study is made, I have run across an excellent sample of one, a former world-class squash player who has run tests on himself and has come to the conclusion that he should abstain from sex for forty-eight hours before a serious match. I asked him to explain how he had arrived at this conclusion.

"Some people say that sex helps your game, but I think that's a lot of baloney. Unless it is an individual difference, which I doubt. I think if a person were to test it scientifically as I have done, he or she would find that the amount of physical effort you can expend after sex is significantly less than before. I have come to this conclusion by taking certain physical tests such as push-ups and sprints, before and after. In addition, before several of the matches that I have lost, prior to my tests, I had violated this principle.

"Naturally, you tend to hear about the exceptional cases, where someone who has just set a new record or played particularly well has had sex beforehand. They are certainly more prone to talk about it than if they had lost. There is a generally held desire to believe that sex and winning are complementary. It titillates people to think so. It's in line with male aspirations and a macho point of view—the 'I don't give a damn' outlook.

"While it is correct to have a certain evenness of temper, so that you can be within your own values while you're playing, you also have to have a certain tension and desire to achieve, a momentum and persistence. I don't think there's any question that after someone has had sex, he or she is pretty tired and relaxed, which is antithetical to one of the major states necessary for victory. For example, try to get into a fever pitch after dallying, unless you dally without consummation, and that's something I haven't explored."

I asked this squash player if he were exploring the matter further and he said, "At my age, one leaves that sort of scientific experimentation to readers of your book and others of an inquisitive nature."

Jansher Khan (Pakistan) and Chris Dittmar (Australia).

10. MATCH PLAY

Author's note: Most of this section was written in the 1970s for my book *Smart Squash: Using Your Head to Win.* Consistent with the title, it deals largely with what goes on inside a player's head during the match. Because very little of it relates to the ball, the court, or even to tactics, it is still relevant. As such, it is a testament to the enduring appeals of squash for the thinking athlete. It is also a testament to the 100-plus years that the hard ball held us all in thrall.

JUST BEFORE A MATCH

After all the hard training and preparation, the day of your match arrives. You are ready in every way. What do you do in the last few hours before you play? Much attention has been paid lately to the ways of preparing your mind and body just before going on the court. It is now clear that the consistent winners, especially at the very top levels of play, adhere strictly to a pre-match routine to achieve their *ideal performance state.*

Tim Bacon, sports psychologist and coach of squash at Smith College, has developed a training program centered on the five basic mental skills of a well-prepared athlete. If you want to play your best squash, you will need to be ready in each of these skill areas:

Relaxation. The ability to be physically and mentally calm.

Confidence. The ability to keep feelings of self-doubt at bay and generate upbeat emotions through positive thinking.

Energization. The ability to be ready by raising physical and mental energies to appropriate levels.

Visualization. The ability to see mental pictures of shots and patterns of play that enhance effectiveness.

Concentration. The ability to block out distractions and focus on your strengths, your opponent's weaknesses, and the two or three keys to winning your upcoming match.

Bob Callahan agrees with the need for these five skills but thinks that each player must develop his own pre-match routine to realize them. "I try to get my players to go on the court an hour before their match and try to hit a little bit of everything. You should make sure your drops feel good, how the boast comes off the wall, what it's like to hit a length and how it bounces, that the cross-court angle is looking good, your serves are doing okay, and you find your range and targets on all your shots.

"Then, when you've got your shots on, broken a sweat and gotten the blood flowing, you should have a nice long stretch that should be very quiet time, ten minutes or so by yourself, absolutely alone. That's the time I would go over in my head, visualize all the situations, seeing myself out there, and my responses to them, get your mind hooked into what to expect and what's about to happen, thinking about the match. Then make sure you stay loose and warm. Stay connected to the job you have to do, don't chit-chat with friends: you need your own time."

Jahangir Khan likes to avoid the hangers-on at the big matches who invariably pester the players. He will sometimes sit with a friend and discuss a few basics to build his concentration and composure. If all else fails, he says, "I have one excellent method of building up concentration in those tense and difficult moments—ten minutes sitting on the toilet! It's relaxing anyway, but it's a splendid place for thinking about what you are going to do. Quite a few players endorse this wonderful strategy. I recommend it."

WARMING UP

What do you do during the warm-up before a match? Can you gain valuable prematch intelligence? How do you go about sizing up your opponent? Here is what Peter Briggs, Goldie Edwards, Cal MacCracken, and Norm Peck advise:

Briggs: "It is totally impossible to learn from a guy by watching him warm up. There are guys who have never lost a warm-up in their life! There are other guys who will purposely look weak on a particular stroke when actually they're not.

"What you are really doing in warming up is personally trying to get loose, get your eye on the ball. It's all personal."

Edwards: "Sometimes if I haven't seen my opponent before and it's a match, I will try to put on a show in the warm-up. I hit hard a lot and try to make an impression on them. I try to hit good-length balls that get the nick and see how they deal with that.

"You get some players who will hit six to themselves and then hit one to you. I think that's not fair. I think you've got to watch this person carefully. Perhaps they might not be fair when it comes to something more significant. So you've got to watch the score, watch if all the balls are up, you know, watch them like a hawk.

"I watch my opponents to see if they let the ball bounce twice in the warm-up. If they do, then I know they are going to be a little bit slow and laissez-faire during the game. Barbara Maltby would never let a ball bounce twice in a warm-up. She knows better than that. You see, you have to get the ball on the one-bounce in the game, and the warm-up is the warm-up for the game. And yet some players regularly let the ball bounce twice. Now they're the ones who aren't going to get to the top. They're just not going to do it. Because that's their whole approach to competitive squash, and it just isn't enough."

MacCracken: "Warm-ups don't have to be those back-and-forth cross-courts to each other all the time. They can have much more purpose. You don't have to give your opponents the same shot every time. You can certainly watch how they hit a backhand versus a forehand, how they hit low versus high shots, how they hit a shot that breaks off the wall, and whether they can pick it off close to the side wall. Then you will be able to plan your game based on their weaknesses."

Peck: "The first thing we tell our players is to avoid generalities based on an opponent's physical make-up. You know, if a player is six-feet-three and two hundred pounds, the obvious generality is that he hits the ball hard and is somewhat clumsy. Or if the player is five-six and a hundred and thirty-five pounds, that he scrambles around and uses a lot of junk shots. But the stereotype doesn't always work. For example, Arif Sarfraz, who is very small, can hit the ball harder than most big players. And Frank Brosens, who is very large, has more touch than most players on our team.

"There *are* some things you can look for in the warm-up that can be helpful. For example, a player who warms up intelligently will oftentimes be a well-coached and fairly intelligent player. He takes his time, hits the ball softly at the beginning, keeps the ball off the tin, and just gets used to the feel of the ball and how it reacts on the court, particularly if it's a strange court. This type of player is likely to hit some smart shots during the course of a match.

"On the other hand, a player who goes into the warm-up and hits the first shot as hard as he can, and all he really does is kind of bang the ball around, hits a lot of tins, hits the ball kind of flat, this type of player will usually play the same kind of game. We have a standing joke that he's warming up his tin shots.

"One of the things we tell each of our players to do, particularly if we are playing an away match and have driven three hours or so, is to go on the court a half hour to forty-five minutes before the match, to hit for fifteen or twenty minutes alone, to really work on his shots, get himself loose, and prepare himself mentally for the match he is about to play."

CHOOSING A GAME PLAN

Squash has been described as physical chess—a game wherein you move opponents around the court with a preplanned series of shots until they are in a weak enough position for you to hit an easy winner.

The chess analogy is apt only up to a point. In squash, instead of a reflective pause between shots, there is a constant interaction between the physical and the mental, and there is no finite number of responses to a shot. In effect, preplanning or strategy can be a sometime thing. It may work during one part of the game and fail at another.

"Consider for a moment what happens in the course of a point," says Norm Peck. "Most players—I'd say ninety-five percent of all the people I've seen play squash—are very predictable in what they do. They will hit the same shot off a given shot just about every time they get it. For example, if I were to hit you a three-wall shot, you will most likely go up and return it cross-court. So I hit that three-wall, and then I can move only halfway back to the T and wait for your cross-court. Then I can just lay that ball back down the line. And if you're not thinking about what you are doing, I'll do this to you all day, and you won't even realize it.

"Or, say that I hit a ball deep to your forehand corner. Most players are taught in the beginning to hit a rail shot if the ball is in the back court. So I hit one into that corner and then I just kind of slide over a half step or so, nothing dramatic, and as soon as the ball leaves your racquet, I take the other half step and cut that rail shot of yours off. And, again, I'll do this over and over, until something goes on in your head that says, 'Maybe I'd better hit cross-court.' So you will surprise me with the first cross-court. But the next time you do that, you'll say, 'The cross-court worked—I'll hit cross-courts off his rails,' and you hit me three, four, five of them, and I'll cut off the next four.

"So it's really a game where you have to be *mentally* a step ahead of the other player."

A game plan should not be too elaborate. It ought to be flexible, permitting you to adjust as play progresses. "The average player should have a few shots he can win points with," says Vic Niederhoffer. "He should vary the frequency with which he tries to hit these shots during the match. Depending on his opponent's stamina and quality of play, he should change the game dynamics and vary the risk/reward ratio."

Peter Briggs avoids picking a game plan until after he has played the first game. "Once you have played him a game, you can pretty much tell: Does the guy move up and back well? Does he volley the ball? How hard does he hit the ball? How close to the tin does he hit the ball?

"Lots of guys are great shooters, but they go very close to the tin, so the way to play them is to keep the ball in play. Sooner or later, they'll just get frustrated and miss.

"There are other guys who have long, fluid strokes, so you volley everything you can get ahold of, and you try to rush them. And if the guy is tall, you try *not* to put him in a position where he will use his reach. Try instead to keep him tangled up in his long arms."

Let's extend Peter Briggs's approach to the type of player you often meet at the beginning levels of league play: the power player who has learned how to hit ground strokes and loves the visceral surge to be derived from hard-hit rails and cross-courts. These players usually do not stroke well above the shoulder level, so the thing to do is keep the ball out of their groove with shots that require volleying.

Another approach to playing ahead is to understand that there are certain shots that will bring a somewhat predictable response. Norm Peck gives a good example of this: "If I hit a forcing cross-court to the left that breaks off behind you, there are only a few things you can do with the ball from back there. You've got to use the side wall to get that ball up to the front court, and I know it's going to end up in the right front corner.

"So as soon as I have hit that shot, I'm paying attention to what you're doing. I've watched you use the side wall and I'm moving up and over even as the ball passes me going to the front wall. So I'm there waiting when the ball arrives, and I can usually just dump it in the right front corner for an easy point."

You qualify as having a game plan if you are patient, play to your own strengths, and avoid trying to hit winners until it is time to do so. This is even more important in soft ball than it is in hard ball. In hard ball, an impatient player tries to hit a winner too early or—the weakness that inspired me to write my first squash book—to hit fancy, exotic shots. These principles, equally true of soft ball, are lucidly analyzed by Vic Niederhoffer:

"The problem of going for exotic shots is a very common one. It is probably the biggest weakness that elementary competitive players have. As in all things, the key to this problem is preparation. Ninety-nine percent of hitting the right shot is being prepared to do so.

"Most times when players hit an exotic shot, they are out of position or are desperate to conserve energy. If your opponents can get to the shot, they are going to make a point on it, plus you're generally going to miss the shot, and furthermore it's just not an effective strategic time to do it.

"And what about the player who gives in to the impulse to pulverize a fat ball? Well, I will simply state that the desire to release tension or end points quickly is antithetical to the complete squash player. When a setup occurs, instead of looking at it as the *end* of a point, you should think of this fat ball as the *beginning* of the end, the prelude to a series of shots which should lead to a position where ultimately you will be able to hit the one shot that gives you a reasonable chance of a winner and almost no chance of a loser. Only then do you try to end the point.

"The whole question of success in developing a game plan, of being capable of understanding and using the strategies of squash, is resolved in your mental attitude toward the game. Are you patient? Do you pay attention to detail? Do you have respect for your own abilities to keep going? If you have these qualities, you have a chance to be a very good player."

IN SQUASH, TWO'S A CROWD

When Hashim Khan first came over to this country, he used to take a big follow-through after a very hard-hitting shot. In the international game, because of the wider court, it isn't as necessary to stand close together. You can give a little more room. So Khan was used to taking a big follow-through.

Diehl Mateer was playing Khan in the semi's of the first national open championship. Cal MacCracken was there and gave this report: "Mateer was determined to win, so he was standing his ground, allowing himself to be hit repeatedly on Khan's follow-through. The racquet head was coming around and hitting Mateer on the leg. I went into the locker room with him after the third game and counted twenty-three welts all up and down his right leg, some still showing the impression of the strings. He eventually lost the match, and Henri Salaun beat Khan in the finals on the following day."

The effects of crowding in squash are not always so damaging, but because of the game's speed and its narrow confines, understanding and being able to cope with the physical proximity of your opponent are crucial to success. This will be especially true as U.S. players learn to use the bigger soft-ball swing while having to play predominantly on the narrow court.

Under most playing conditions, crowding is a state of mind that does not include physical contact or even a let call. It is rather a discomfort or stress that players feel when preparing to swing that causes them to hit a slightly rushed or cramped shot. As Peter Briggs says, "There's a difference between playing competitively close to a guy, so you can reach his better shots, and downright hanging all over him. By playing him close, it also adds a little bit more intensity. Lots of guys personally don't like this, your breathing down their necks. It bugs them."

Diehl Mateer not only got close to his opponents when they were hitting; he also knew how to keep them away when it was his turn. Again, MacCracken is the observer: "When you go in against Mateer, he takes his room to take his shot. There's nothing wrong with that. It's perfectly legal. And you *give* it to him. He sticks his rear end *way* out and you find yourself backed flat against the wall when you don't want to be over there. And you wouldn't be over there with most other players because they wouldn't be taking any more room than they actually needed."

A common mistake caused by crowding occurs when you are backing into an area being vacated by your opponent. You have a good bead on the ball but you take your eye off it to see if the way is clear. Now you've got to rebead before hitting and as a result you miss your shot. "There is no reason for this," says Betty Constable, former national women's champion and first coach of women's squash at Princeton University. "You're *not* supposed to be thinking about your opponent. It's just between you and the ball. You have enough work to do to think about that ball and what you're going to do with it."

There are players who take unfair advantage of the court space. They push you around. After a certain amount of this, you have to call "let" and replay the point or you will lose. With players who take up too much of the court space, you've got to train yourself to call let *before* you hit the shot. That's rather hard for a lot of people to do. They can't make the decision that they are being interfered with *fast* enough. It all happens in a fraction of a second, and if you don't call let you are giving your opponent the advantage. The good players don't hit balls even when they are only *mildly* interfered with. They don't hit until their opponent starts adhering to the rules.

When your opponent unnecessarily or continually interferes with your shots, you should ask for a let point, known as a "stroke" in soft ball. Vic Niederhoffer is in favor of awarding let points even when a player has hit a bad shot and is *unable* to clear. "It will *improve* the game, because most of the time I have found a very strange thing: as soon as my opponent has had one let point called against him, he clears ten times better than before. Most of the time when he is in the way, he's doing it because he's a little tired and it requires too much effort to get out of the way. If he's penalized, then all of a sudden the game opens up and you can play squash."

Let points are a product of the 15-point scoring system where a point is won at the end of each rally. Soft-ball exhibitions and many soft-ball tournaments are adopting 15-point scoring to shorten match times and heighten spectator interest. However, the majority of soft-ball matches continue to be played using the international 9-point scoring system where you can win points only when you're serving.

So in situations of possible interference in the 9-point system, a referee can:

1) call "no let," where no interference is judged to have occurred, and the result of the rally stands,

2) call "let," when interference occurred and the obstructed player could have made a good return and was trying to do so, causing the rally to be replayed, or

3) award a "stroke" to the obstructed player, when the conditions for a let apply and the obstructing player was *not* trying to get out of the way, or when the obstructed player was in a position to hit a winning shot (even when the obstructing player is trying to get out of the way). The player who is awarded a stroke wins a point if he is the server or wins the serve if he is the receiver.

It is remarkable how many soft-ball rallies end with a stroke being awarded to the obstructed player. If your opponent crowds you or hinders your swing at all—for example, if you hit him with your backswing or follow-through—he loses the rally. In hard ball, you could get much closer to your opponent without having a let point called. In soft ball, you have to be more careful about crowding. Likewise, if you hit a weak ball, you need to be very keen on clearing or you lose the rally.

David Pearson, the British coach, revealed a shrewd tactic that most ex-hard-ballers take a long time to learn because they are so used to hitting with a compact swing. Hard-ball players tend to cock their wrist and pull the racquet back close to the body, and this gives the opponent room, particularly in a wide court, to slide around and get in position to cover the short shots. David recommends in this situation that you take your racquet back from your body horizontally as a "fence" to keep your opponent behind you until you are ready to play your short shot.

DECEPTION IS THE ESSENCE OF SQUASH

Of all the racquet games, squash is the trickiest. Many points end with an opponent scurrying away from where the ball has actually been aimed. Deception won the point. It follows therefore that squash is the most challenging mentally of all racquet sports. Some would go even further and say, of any physical contest.

In a recent match between Brett Martin and Peter Marshall during the 1994 Lehman Brothers Tournament of Champions, Paul Assaiante observed to me as we were sitting together in the stands: "What Martin started to do in the middle of that game was he started to hold a bunch of balls and change tempos. He was waiting, delaying the stroke, hitting some low, hard forehands. He does a lot of fades, he'll hold the ball, turn his shoulders away from the rail, and then hit the ball down the rail. So he's not only trying to keep Marshall running up and back, he's also trying to keep him off balance by changing tempos, fading, and faking. Whereas Marshall almost never fakes. What he shows is what he hits."

Bob Callahan believes that the key to deception is early racquet preparation. "The racquet preparation position is what telegraphs the shot, so your racquet has to be up, ready, and stopped, so there are no cues to read."

Richard Hankinson, assistant coach of the women's team at Princeton University, commented on the importance of deception in soft ball: "One of the real differences that we've got to focus on more and more with the women is the ability with the soft ball to hold your shot and force your opponent to commit. If there are two or three shot choices you can make from a given setup, the longer you can hold your stroke, the more chance that your opponent will guess and move before you strike."

Contrasting deception between hard ball and soft ball, Paul Assaiante thinks one of the biggest differences occurs in the front court: "In hard ball, we used to go to the front wall with the racquet very low and extended out in front of our bodies, then we could hit an accurate drop shot or corner shot, or from that same low position you could still generate enough power to hit a deep rail. In soft ball, you cannot do this; going up with a low racquet is too predictable, you must go to the front wall with the racquet very high, and from that position you can hit a ball deep or decelerate the head and execute a drop shot—it allows you to blend your shotmaking."

In the larger context of racquet sports, Cal MacCracken, who has played a lot of tennis as well as squash, explains why deception is the essence of squash: "The biggest difference to me is that in squash *deception* is an *extremely* important part of the game. You have to learn to hit your basic shots with the view from your rear end looking the same. That you learn by *yourself* in playing alone in a court and rallying. You make *sure* that you hit all of your shots with your feet the same way.

"When you don't play a great deal, you begin to give clues as to what shot you're hitting, and you no longer have the element of surprise on your side. Your opponent knows what you're doing. An observant opponent watches you all of the time and knows what shot you're getting ready to hit. You signal this with your feet, racquet, hands, and body.

"The great players I have played against tried to deceive me in every way as to the shot they were going to hit. A typical example of that was Jack Summers, pro at M.I.T., who was national professional champion. I used to watch him play Sherman Howes from Boston. Howes was a tremendous power hitter. He could hit the ball so hard you'd think it was going right through the wall. Howes was champion of the Boston area at that time. He'd come up to Summers, who was twenty-five to thirty years older than he was, and he'd say, 'Five dollars on this game.' So they'd play and Howes would win, and then he'd win the second game and Summers would be down ten bucks. Then Summers would say, 'Double or nothing on this,' and would win the next three in a row with the most amazing deceptions. Howes would just stand there thinking the ball was going one way and it would go the other.

"All things being equal, and maybe even when they're a little unequal, I'd put my money on a deceptive player every time."

FOCUSING ON THE SCORE

I have heard that Bob Hetherington, a former Yale star who held a national ranking for many years, sometimes sealed himself off from the match score so completely that he would in effect be playing as many as 175 isolated points, the equivalent of a five-game match in which the score in each game goes to 18-17. He thus canceled out the condition of being ahead or behind, which in turn made it impossible for the score to have any effect on the quality of his play during a given point. It is said that he sometimes had to be told when the match was over.

Of course, Hetherington-like powers of concentration, which were known to be awesome, have not been generally bestowed, so that most players have developed playing habits based on the score. Are they well ahead? Are they behind 10-2 in the third? Is it 13-all in the fifth? What do they do in these situations?

Consciousness of the score seems to vary a great deal with individual players. For example, I asked Cal MacCracken whether he played conservatively or aggressively if he was leading by a large margin. He said, "Never change a winning game. To show you what can happen, I had an experience in 1948, when I was first starting to break into the national scene. I was playing Charlie Brinton, four-time winner of the national championships, and still defending champion, in the quarterfinals of the nationals at the Harvard Club in Boston. I won the first two games fairly easily, like ten and nine, and then in the third game, I had him 14-7, and believe it or not, I lost that game!

"Andy Ingraham spoke to me in the locker room before the fourth game. He said, 'Cal, don't change your game. Keep it exactly the way it was in the first, second, and beginning of the third game. You got panicky trying for that last point and changed it all around. Go back in there and play your standard game.' I did, and I won it about 15-10. So I beat the national champ. That was my first real important victory."

On the other hand, if Goldie Edwards is ahead by a large margin, she will sometimes play a little bit of cat-and-mouse with her opponent. "I guess it's really a bad thing," she says, "if winning is the only criterion. But I like to have fun, so I play to see how much I can make them run. I get tremendous satisfaction in putting the ball exactly where I want to put it. So I will do lobs and drops just to keep it in play, just for the sake of keeping the point going. And I must admit I do that sometimes when I should be paying more attention to winning the point as soon as I can."

The 9-point international scoring system encourages a more conservative style of play on the serve and return of serve. It is much harder to score an ace on the serve than it was with the hard ball. Add to that the fact that you only get one serve and you only score when you have the serve, and you come up with the rationale for conservative serving. It is not uncommon in the international scoring system, according to Paul Assaiante, "to see an entire game where nobody does anything on the return of serve but push it down the wall or break a wide cross-court."

One approach to the score if you are ahead, say 2-1, it's the fourth game, and you get down by a large margin, is to save yourself for the last game. Certainly you wouldn't try desperately to get balls and risk tiring yourself. You could even try some ridiculous shots that you would not ordinarily attempt in a match. With the pressure off temporarily, you might make a few of them. If you don't, it doesn't matter. But if you do, it can rattle your opponent, which could be just what you need to make a good start in the fifth game.

On choosing set points to break a tie game, there seems to be more agreement. The better player, the player who is stronger, should choose the greater number of points. The player who is the underdog, who is more tired, and can win only by luck or chance, should choose "no set" (no additional points). An exception to this might occur if your opponent had run off five or six points to catch you at 14-all. You might in that case take advantage of a possible temporary letup and force them to play yet another game point.

Momentum is a big factor in squash, perhaps more so than in other racquet sports, because you are given less time and space to compose yourself and dredge up from a slump. As Cal notes, "I think things go in streaks. They certainly do for me." The same is true for Goldie: "I find that if my shots are on, I have great confidence in them, and I play them, and then I'll win a round of points. But as soon as I get nervous and tighten up, or lose confidence in my shots, then it's gone."

Gaining perspective on the score is a good way to shore up your game if things are running against you. It can also be useful so that you don't get carried away with your own prowess and fall into a pit of neglect. Goldie has an interesting way of keeping her head about the score toward the end of a game: "At 12-9 or 9-12, I think of it immediately as being a 3-3 game. You know, three points will finish it off, or three points will tie it. So if I'm up to 12-8, that's a 3-4 situation. That point doesn't pass me, especially if it's 9-12 or closer, without my thinking about it.

In fact, sometimes I've even been tempted to say to my opponent, 'Okay now, that's a 3-3 situation,' but I don't."

CONTROLLING YOUR MIND ON THE COURT

I still cringe when I remember the days of hot-blooded competition in the New York City D league and the times when I let my mind interfere with my natural abilities. On one occasion, I had just come from a city D singles match that went to five games, three of which were overtime. I was leading 11-7 in the fifth, and I guess I thought the match was in the bag. It wasn't. My opponent won the next eight points and the match.

Again, I remember the time when we took our club players down to play the undergraduates at Princeton. After my regular match, I played a pickup game with Nancy Gengler, then the women's intercollegiate champion and stalwart, along with Amy Knox, of the Princeton women's team. We were both playing well, I with some forcing cross-courts and rails, she with some beautiful gets and touch shots, and then we arrived at 13-all. Nancy chose five-out-of-nine as a tiebreaker. On the next point we got into an extended rally until she hit a deep ball that broke off the right wall and came off the back wall slightly to the left of center. I backed up on it and really *whanged* one—right into her fanny.

Until that moment the sex thing had not entered my head. But there I stood, feeling awful and thinking of the round red mark with the small white center welling up there under the shorts of this fragile Princeton coed. We played a let and Nancy proceeded to win the next five points and the game.

What can happen to an athlete's mind in mid-contest is magnified in the game of squash. In terms of the time available to react, position, and stroke, it is the fastest of racquet sports, with the added challenge of contending with another body for the same space. All these characteristics place a huge premium on the ability to maintain concentration.

You are there, in the confines of a small white room. The ball is streaking up and down the rails. You move to the T, retreat to the corner, squeeze around your opponent and go back to the T. "That's why the game is unique," says Peter Briggs. "It's like boxing because of its closeness and intensity. Both players are physically contained. There's nowhere to go. You can look anywhere you want and all you see is walls or the other guy. Or the gallery. And there's no solace from the gallery, because they're just a sea of faces staring down at you."

To counteract this intensity and confinement, Peter tries to maintain a sense of detachment during a match. "If anything," he says, "I would tend to keep a very good humor on the court. Maybe crack a couple of jokes. I do this because in the end you have to keep things in perspective. You've got to realize basically the total inaneness of what you are doing. Scurrying around in a white room chasing a small black ball. I'm fully aware of that all the time. That's why I can go into the court and, whether I win or lose, I forget about it once I'm out of the court. I find a guy who takes this totally seriously a little bit amusing. Everything, even the most serious squash match, needs tempering."

So you learn to do it for yourself, to stay even-tempered, to hold off distractions, to play at your best level throughout the match. How you do this is, again, a very personal matter, subject to great variation, both among individual players and from match to match.

The year that all four semifinalists at the women's national intercollegiates were Princetonians, Betty Constable's players were termed "ice goddesses" by the press because of their steely powers of concentration. She had taught them, "None of this gallery stuff. *Never* look in the gallery. It's too distracting. The moment you look in the gallery your concentration goes. You've got a lot of work to do in that court. The only person you ever look at is the referee, to ask for a let. Once you look beyond and see a friend or someone else, you've lost two points. How're you going to get your mind back? The game's too fast."

Cal MacCracken's approach is to concentrate on his opponent's weakness. "If you will analytically try to study what the other person's weakness is, then you concentrate on that and forget your own problems and errors. You do two things this way: you obviously improve because you do better if you continually press opponents by hitting to their weakness, but the main thing is that you take your mind off yourself, and that usually overcomes panic."

Cal observed that you can also be distracted by an opponent's injury. He recalled the time he was playing Henri Salaun, and Salaun twisted his knee. "He lay on his back moaning—after I had won the first two games and was leading him ten to three in the third. I really thought he would never walk again. I thought his leg was permanently injured. It seemed that bad. He got up and said in his heavy French accent, 'I theenk I cahn plah-ee.' Salaun then got fifteen out of the next sixteen points and beat me easily in the fourth and fifth games."

No matter how successful you are at controlling your mind, there will be bad days and momentary lapses during a match. "On some days," says Goldie Edwards, "I feel more aggressive than others. I assert myself, get out front and take the upper hand, and cream the ball. On those days, it's important and easy. On other days, I don't have the energy, I just don't care. I nip about at the back and fiddle around.

"If it is a big match and I feel myself slipping, I try to think thoughts of how important it is. I try to relax. I take a deep breath and just let my muscles go, to untense. When receiving the serve, I try to keep a firm grip but a loose arm. A tight arm moves more slowly.

"I try to create a positive feeling that I can do it. I recall previous wins over this same opponent, and over better opponents. There have been times when I thought, 'Well, too bad, this one is gone,' then I relaxed and ended up winning. I remember the time I was down love-two in the Canadian Open against Jane Dixon. Somebody came down and said, 'What you need to do is hit higher shots that break off the walls and keep her going to the back. I did and it worked. I came back and won the next three games. When you're in the heat of a match, it's hard to see everything that is happening. Having the ability to do that for yourself would be marvelous."

At the top levels of the game, players are known for their abilities to block out everything that doesn't bear on winning. Vic Niederhoffer has a remarkable view of mental control: "I've never had a problem controlling myself. The sport is supposed to be an expression of your personality and your values. By allowing your values to be upset on the court, you are just losing your dignity and becoming less of a person *on* the court than you are *off* the court.

"There is certainly no reason for you to get out of control in the court more than is appropriate in life itself. You should have a general feeling that you are going to concentrate on two or three different things during the game—the ways you can win points and how you should vary the risks that you take during the game. That's probably the thing that you should change the most: how fast you want to end the points, and what type of shots you think are worthy of risk."

Jahangir Khan (Pakistan), foreground, and Gary Waite (Canada).

11. PARTING SHOTS

RANDOM NUGGETS OF WISDOM

In my approach to this book, I have tried to present only what would be useful to my readers, and to do so with brevity. Several valuable but random ideas that found no natural place in the flow of sections are included here, followed by a summary of what I think is most important if you want to improve at soft-ball squash and consistently play your best game.

When to change the ball. When the ball gets old, it "slicks up" and plays differently. Frank Satterthwaite uses what he calls "the squeak test" to tell when you should turn in the ball: "Take a dry ball and rub it on glass, if it squeaks, it's still okay. When it doesn't squeak any more, it's not gripping. You can certainly play with it but it will not have the same properties that you want from a fresh ball."

Soft-ball shots not often seen in hard ball. The lob, working boast, and volley cross-court nick are three shots that are rarely seen in hard ball but are an integral part of the soft-ball game. A lob with the soft ball may be hit with a much greater range of force than with the hard ball and can be most effective both offensively and defensively. The working boast is a relatively easy shot to learn and is a key shot for moving and tiring your opponent or for winning points outright. The volley cross-court nick is a favorite of advanced players for ending the rally when presented with a loose ball sort of high and in the center.

Soft-ball shots on wide versus narrow courts. It may be obvious, but players switching to the wide court seemingly refuse to use its width properly. They need to hit more cross-courts and working boasts to benefit from the extra 2 1/2 feet. On the narrow court, the soft ball presents new opportunities not available with the hard ball: hit more drop shots when you are in front of your opponent, and use the high straight lob to take advantage of the higher out-of-court lines—both shots are deadly on the narrow court.

What's your strongest deep shot? Because it is so critical to put your opponent deep in the corners, you should know and use your best deep shots. Jay Nelson figures it this way: "How do I most frequently try to get a guy deep in the court? On the forehand, it's probably the cross-court, on the backhand side it's the rail, and they both end up in the same spot. So, I'm trying to get the guy into that back left corner. I think my forehand rail is better than my backhand cross-court, my weakest of the four deep shots is the backhand cross-court, and of the four strokes, my backhand rail is probably my best."

Is the backhand or forehand a more natural shot? The backhand rail is hit more naturally because your arm wraps around your body on the backswing and comes to a controlled stopping point each time, whereas the forehand backswing is floating somewhere out beyond your body, taking more practice and precision to gain the same consistent result. The forehand pronates more readily and thus tends to produce a cross-court. When lining up your body to hit a shot, you tend to hit a forehand from a more open stance and therefore to hit cross-courts.

On hitting a beautiful ball. While Ned Edwards and I were watching the first round of the 1994 Lehman Brothers Tournament of Champions, he said, "To me a lot of these guys in the early rounds don't hit the ball fine. They're just out there working. The ball's being hit back and forth and they should just put on running shoes and say, 'Let's have a trot here for a while.' I think they're passing up the chance to hit a beautiful ball."

Jansher Khan puts technique above fitness. As described by Satinder Bajwa, Jansher's North American manager, "Jansher gradually worked up to beating Rod Eyles in the world juniors, then won the world title in '87, beating Jahangir in the semis and Dittmar in the finals. At that time, his game relied on running, not volleying, but letting the ball go to the back wall—attritional play. Now he attacks more, focuses on cutting the ball off. As much as people like to think of soft ball as a fitness game, Jansher has spent more time working on his attacking and stroke play than on his attritional side. It has paid off because he attacks well, he finishes a ball well."

The importance of positioning. It is much easier to learn the shots than it is to get in position to make them. Once you are in position, the stroke is always the same, but getting there can take a thousand variations. If you are out of position, you can have the best forehand in town and it won't do you any good.

Backing on the ball. Betty Constable gives this advice to get you in position to hit a ball that has angled off the side wall and is being hit off the rear wall: "You never move back and stop and freeze your feet to the floor. By doing that you've committed yourself. You should always be moving so that at the last minute you step back into the ball. This way you hit it while you're moving forward and everything comes down at once. Your foot comes down and your racquet comes down to hit the ball.

"To get a ball like that, the moment you know it is going to come around and off the back wall, you should follow the ball with your racquet, like a pointer. It's a smooth, rhythmic way of getting your racquet back."

Turning should be avoided. Given a choice of turning with a sharply angled ball or backing to strike it on the side it was hit, you should always back on the ball. It is much safer and it forces your opponent over to the wall, giving you nearly the whole court and a variety of options for a winning shot.

Watching your opponent. When watching your opponent behind you, keep your feet well spread and parallel to the front wall. Turn *only* the top part of your body to watch. That way you can push off in either direction to retrieve a shot. Two common errors made in this situation are turning your feet toward your opponent, which prevents you from getting around quick enough for a cross-court shot, and having your feet together, which keeps you from being able to push off quickly in any direction.

The resurgence of club lessons. The switch to soft ball has breathed new life into the teaching programs of squash professionals. Craig Thorpe-Clark sees "a reawakening of the junior programs and club lessons. The new ball and the realization that there's a whole new game and regimen to learn has given the coaches and club pros something significant to offer. And the players themselves realize that they'd better take lessons or they won't learn properly. The soft-ball game has created a big new market."

Using video tape. There is no way to duplicate video tape's instant replay and stop-action capability through other teaching alternatives. The mental images thus conveyed of one's own strokes and court mannerisms are a valuable input for use in mental practice as well as on-court practice.

Fair play. What do you do if your opponent keeps playing shots after the second bounce? Vic Niederhoffer has an approach that I like. "You have to realize that if you want to be a good sport, it's a personal thing. You shouldn't worry about your opponent. That's his business. To hold a grudge because the other person is cheating and you're not is really not very mature.

"Tell your opponent he's hitting them on two bounces. The main thing to understand is that very often your opponent doesn't realize the ball has bounced twice. You have to be pretty good to really know what you're doing wrong in this game. Most players, when they are told they got it on two bounces, will be pleased to play the point over. Which is the fair thing to do. The worst thing to do is dwell on it with an envious feeling that they're getting away with something that you're not getting away with.

"If that doesn't work, ask for a referee, and if you go that way, then neither of you calls anything on yourself. Let the referee make all the decisions."

Being prepared. Again, I credit the wisdom of Vic Niederhoffer: "If there is any key to winning, it lies in preparation. Preparation comes many months before your match, when you're running around the track or practicing hundreds of three-wall nicks. If you're not tired and you're in an equilibrium position where you are strong near the end, then you can hit shots offensively rather than defensively, and develop your game within a more competitive framework. You will have more respect for your own abilities to keep going. You will be more resilient in defeat, and more worthy in victory."

■　■　■

Although I believe there is food for thought in this book even for the finest players, I set out with the goal of creating a regimen for those who are trying to convert from hard ball to soft ball, or who are trying to learn soft-ball squash for the first time.

With that goal in mind, I will summarize six areas to concentrate on that will help you realize your potential as a soft-ball player and, from match to match, to play your best game.

SIX ESSENTIALS FOR YOUR BEST GAME

1. Learn the soft-ball stroke. This is no bed of roses. Even Demer Holleran says it took her some two years to convert from the short, punchy stroke of a hard-baller to the full-throated swing of a soft-baller. If you can just get your racquet into the high starting position, more than half the problem will be solved. From there it is a gravity and momentum thing, with emphasis on a full follow-through to the target on the front wall, then up to the other end of the big "U." Drilling and work with a professional are both essential to acquire and muscle-memorize the classic soft-ball stroke.

2. Move on an arc into shooting position. This too, if you are unlearning, is a bitch. Two needs dictate the curved path—striking the ball side-on well away from your body, and stretching into that position with one foot still "on the carpet" (an imaginary rectangle in the center of the court) so you can rebound quickly to the T.

Ghosting—the squash player's equivalent of solo dance practice—is the best way to work out foot patterns and imagined shot sequences while moving on a curved path into shooting position.

3. Do the shot drills. There is no substitute for practicing your shots, nor anything that pays as big a return. The top players do it regularly to keep their racquet work sharp. A big advantage of squash and its "little white room" is the ease of setting up repetitive routines where the ball comes back to you so you can go wild practicing the basic shots: rails, cross-courts, boasts, lobs, and drops. Hit them as volleys and as ground strokes and try to increase the number of repetitions while striving for accuracy. And be sure to practice the serve, both lob and hard, from both sides.

4. Maintain your fitness. This is individually determined based on your competitive level. At a minimum, to enjoy club matches without having fatigue erode your shot production in the later games, you should do some stretching and strengthening work two or three times a week. Just a few weights, some aerobics on the machines, and several six-point drills for anaerobics will maintain a nice competitive edge in your game.

5. Plan your match. Think about who and where you're going to play. What have you been emphasizing in practice as your key weapons? What are your opponent's strong and weak points? Allow enough time to warm up and stretch before going on the court. Get your eye on the ball with the basic shots during the warm-up. Stay focused on the one or two things you need to do to win points.

6. Cultivate a soft-baller's mentality. This reduces to the simple discipline of waiting until you have an opening to try and finish the point. Again, this is difficult for ex-hard-ballers who could win points by shooting just about anytime and from about anywhere on the court. I can think of no better way to define this discipline properly than by paraphrasing St. Paul's letter to the Corinthians: "Though I have fitness, technique, strategy, these three, but have not *patience*, I am nothing."

GLOSSARY OF SQUASH TERMS

Ace: an outright winner on the serve, where the receiver does not even make contact with the ball.

Back-wall boast: a desperate, last-chance shot hit into the back wall after a ball has passed you, with the hope it will return to the front wall on the fly.

Board: an angled piece of wood painted red (the lowest line on the front wall) to which the tin is attached. Hitting the board or the tin with the ball ends the rally.

Boast: a shot unique to squash, where the ball is first hit into the side or rear wall, and perhaps hits other walls before hitting the front wall.

Chassé: a gliding step in which one foot is kept in advance of the other, used when moving sideways, for example after a forehand serve from the righthand box.

Cross-court: a shot hit to angle from one side to the other, hitting the side wall a little behind your opponent so that it forces him to go back for the retrieve.

Cut line: the line on the front wall six feet above the floor, above which a good serve must hit.

Defensive boast: a shot hit from deep in a corner, hit with medium pace and a lofting stroke to buy time and keep the ball in play, usually not recommended if the player can get behind the ball and hit a rail.

Die: a ball that bounces twice is "dead," ending the rally; it may also hit the nick and roll out, known as "dying in the nick."

Down: a Marker's call to indicate the end of a rally when an otherwise good serve or return has hit the tin, failed to reach the front wall, bounced twice on the floor, or hit a player before bouncing twice.

Drive: a forcefully hit ground stroke aimed to rebound off the front wall into one of the rear corners, with either a straight drive or a cross-court drive.

Drop shot: a ball hit softly and low onto the front wall; a straight drop is aimed so it comes in close to the side wall and is difficult to return, a cross-court drop is hit at a wide angle to "wrong-foot" an opponent leaning towards what he thinks is going to be a straight drop.

Fault: a bad serve, hit too low onto the front wall, into the tin, short of the service quarter, out of court, or that fails to reach the front wall first.

Foot fault: a serve hit when at least one of the server's feet is not touching the floor within the service box, clear of the red line.

Game ball: called by the Marker when the server needs one point to win the game.

Get: the successful return of a difficult shot, as in "good get!"

Half-court line: the line parallel to the side walls that divides the rear court into two equal service quarters, and that intersects the short line to form the T.

Half-time: mid-point in the five-minute warm-up period before a match, called by the Referee.

Hand: duration of the server's time at serve.

Hand out: called by the Marker when a change of server occurs.

Kill: usually a volley of a loose shot, hit low onto the front wall close to the side wall to die in the nick.

Length: hitting a shot deep to the rear corners; hitting "to a length" is preferred British style, where Americans would say "a deep ball." Good length (or depth) is a shot that reaches the back wall and barely plops off to die.

Let: the replaying of a rally due to excusable interference.

Let point: in the 15-point scoring system, where a point is won on each rally, a let point may be awarded by the Referee to a player who has been interfered with.

Lob: a ball hit high onto the front wall so it rebounds in a high, looping arc into one of the rear corners; you can hit a cross-court lob or a straight lob down the rail.

Loose shot: a ball that is not well hit and comes back towards the center of the court, giving the incoming striker a good chance to hit a winner.

Marker: one of two officials controlling a match, the Marker calls the score, service faults, balls that are "not up" or out of court, and repeats the calls of the Referee.

Match ball: called by the Marker when the server needs one point to win the match.

Nick: another term unique to squash, where a ball hits exactly in the intersection of the wall and the floor, rolling out on the floor for a winner.

No set: the call made by a player whose opponent has just scored a point to tie the score at 8-all or 14-all, meaning that the game will end with the scoring of one more point.

Not up: called by the Marker when the ball is struck incorrectly by server or striker, when it bounces twice before being hit, or when it touches the striker.

Out-of-court line: the continuous line marking the top boundaries of the court.

Philadelphia: an unorthodox shot preferred at odd moments to throw off your opponent, it is hit from a wide angle very high up and tight into the corner on the front wall, it rebounds as a cross-court lob and, when perfectly hit, comes off the other side wall almost parallel to the back wall—very difficult to hit and to return.

Rail: American usage for a ball hit parallel to the side wall, deep into the corner; British usage prefers "straight drive."

Rally: a serve only (if not returned) or any number of exchanges of the ball, ending when the ball ceases to be in play.

Redrop: to hit a drop shot following your opponent's drop shot.

Referee: one of two officials controlling a match, the Referee allows or disallows lets, awards strokes, calls the time, calls "stop" to stop play when warranted, gives conduct warnings, and awards conduct points, games, or the entire match in cases of egregiously bad conduct. The Referee decides all appeals and his decision is final.

Reverse corner: a shot associated with the hard-ball game, hit from the side of the court at a wide angle into the opposite side wall and then the front wall.

Service box: the two 5'3" squares in which the server must stand when hitting the serve.

Service quarter: the two equal halves of the rear court, into which the server alternately must bounce the serve, unless volleyed first.

Shape: a player shapes when he takes the proper stance and prepares his racquet to hit a given shot, e.g. *he shaped for a straight drive;* also "show," as in *he showed a rail but hit a trickle boast.*

Shooter: a player who is good at or has a tendency to go for winners, which in soft ball can be a handicap.

Short line: the line 18 feet back from and parallel to the front wall that intersects the half-court line to form the T, behind which a good serve must bounce or be "short."

Skid boast: a shot hit as a surprise from the same position as a defensive boast from the rear corner, it requires top skills to hit it high and far forward onto the side wall, then to the front where it rebounds like a cross-court lob.

Striker: the player whose turn it is to hit the ball.

Stroke: a) used synonymously with "swing"; b) in the 9-point scoring system where points are won only by the server, "winning a stroke" means that a player wins the rally. In the case of interference, the Referee may award a penalty stroke to the player interfered with.

T: literally, the intersection of the short and half-court lines; as used in play, the T is a small zone in the center of the court where you want to be standing soon after having hit a good deep ball—to control the T is to control the match.

Tin: the apron of metal attached to the "board," it descends vertically to touch the floor, covers the full width of the court, and when hit by the ball, produces a tinny sound announcing the end of the rally. Sometimes also called the "telltale." Modern tins are bent, thus eliminating the board.

Trickle boast: a shot hit from up front as a deceptive alternative to a drop shot or a deep rail, it is hit sharply into the side wall so it angles widely across the front of the court.

Turning: when a ball has been hit along, say, the backhand side but angles sharply off the wall and rear of the court, the receiving player has a choice of "turning" to take the ball on his forehand, a maneuver that often results in a let. The player who does so must call "turning" or "coming around" to warn his opponent.

Volley: striking the ball in mid-air before it has bounced; volleying in soft ball is much more important than it was in hard ball.

Winner: a winning shot, and a winning shooter.

Working boast: a frequently hit shot designed to move your opponent to the front of the court, causing him "to bust his butt chasing after it."

I N D E X